Contents

Steaming through the NHS— time for the profession to unite

Stephen Lock *Editor, BMJ*

One conspicuous feature of the NHS white paper and its working papers has been the lack of detail. In a series of editorials and commissioned articles by experts the BMJ has attempted to explore some of the implications; the articles have been grouped by topic but are otherwise unchanged, apart from an added editorial summary.

All ages have their fashions and in crime today's is "steaming": a gang runs amok through a crowded train or carnival demanding money at knifepoint. The aim is achieved through bewilderment and fear, much as in Clausewitz's description of total war.

The government has used a comparable strategy as one of the two prongs in imposing its plans for the fourth reorganisation of the health service. Announced initially by the Prime Minister on television, the inquiry's remit, conduct, and input remain undisclosed (as did the membership of the Cabinet committee). Thereafter communication has been sharp and in public: a series of synchronised and accurate leaks to the press beforehand; a razmattaz media launch; and an inordinately short timetable for the professions' responses.

These new proposals need to be seen in the political perspective. Having curbed the power of the industrial trades unions, the government is now tackling the power of the professions—schoolteachers, academics, and lawyers. In planning the reform of the last, for example, there was a similar lack of contributions by professionals: no solicitor, barrister, or judge was consulted. Moreover, once such plans have gone public the second prong of the government's attack is to deride any professional complaints; in the case of the NHS, we are told, these come from Luddites, a BMA that is out of touch with its members and that has opposed any projected change in the NHS in the past 40 years.

As was evidently intended, the proposals in *Working for Patients* are difficult to debate; to the shallowness of the original rhetoric has been added that of the working papers, which lack any detail. But some comment is possible. Already it is clear that the necessary skills, equipment, and experience for the envisaged information systems are not available; that few experiments have been done (and those that have are not complete); and that no pilot trials are proposed (as was suggested by Alain Enthoven, the guru of NHS reform by management). Doctors are convinced that the proposals are likely to lead to a two tier structure—in both hospitals and general practice. Add to this the ignoring of the vital aspects of research, training, and community care, and the politicisation of all levels from the Secretary of State downwards and it is not fanciful to talk about the end of the traditional health service, with its low administrative costs and its decent principle of uniform access to a high standard of medical care. And at a time when large scale privatisation is underway can that of the NHS be far behind, given that the proposed new structures, such as budget holding practices and independent hospitals, make it almost axiomatic that they behave like commercial enterprises.

Nobody should lose sight of why the whole exercise started: mounting concern at the funding crises in the acute sector, typified by cancelled operations, such as cardiac surgery on children. This led to protests by both the public and the profession, with the presidents of the three major royal colleges seeing the Prime Minister. None of this crisis will be diminished by the white paper's proposals. There is no more money— indeed, there will probably be less given the heavy expenditure on administration and information systems. All that has happened is to transfer responsibility for the health service's failings from the centre to the periphery, a device to shield the government from public anger and to divert attention from the salient fact: Britain spends proportionately far less on health than its civilised neighbours.

Clearly Mr Clarke has based his strategy on a study of history, aiming at avoiding the "mistakes" of his predecessors Aneurin Bevan, Kenneth Robinson, and Barbara Castle, who he sees as having given in to the unjustified and importunate demands of the doctors. (And if Bevan stuffed consultants' mouths with the gold of merit awards, Clarke seems intent on ingratiating the managers with the silver of opting out.) We should contrast the long drawn out planning of the health service—from 1936 to 1948—with expert advice and widespread consultation, with this administration's year of secret discussions and little consultation. Initially, it has to be said, Clarke has made the running. Public opinion polls suggest some disquiet but the picture is now so complex and confused that few outside the NHS appreciate just how far it will decline

> "... *a series of synchronised and accurate leaks to the press beforehand; a razmattaz media launch; and an inordinately short timetable for the professions' responses.*"

from its present level. Even the debate in the House of Lords showed a disappointing appreciation of the facts and how far rhetoric had triumphed over realism.

The profession, already portrayed by the government's propaganda machine as reactionary and stubborn, should also learn from history. It is little use, for instance, trying to counter a blitzkrieg with intellectual

A return to the poor law? Eventide: a scene in the Westminster Union by Hubert von Herkomer, 1878.

arguments—conceding that parts indeed of the white paper are excellent, objecting that some of them are already being introduced by the profession, and pointing to the disaster many years ago when an untried computer system was imposed on an unprepared London teaching hospital.

But doctors and nurses do have some ammunition. No health service can be run without the cooperation of all the health professions: a total refusal, for example, to implement the proposals for general practice budget holding and hospital opting out would negate much of the enterprise. The public must be told repeatedly about the likely consequences of the proposals, and the BMA council has launched this exercise. And negotiation must take place—and on equal terms, with flexibility and without the duress of a short timetable which owes more to political expediency than to the issues at stake.

In the negotiations the BMA and the royal colleges must speak with one voice, for any seeming division will be exploited to the full. The proliferation of colleges and faculties since 1948 makes this even more difficult, and so far their voice has not been heard. But it is important that the colleges should find tough and skilled leaders of the calibre of Webb-Johnson and Moran; after all was it not Bevan who said that under their charters the royal colleges had the duty of advising the government of the day? The British public and the health professions deserve better than a return to the poor law; though normally both the BMA and the colleges and faculties have separate roles, on this occasion they must stand together.

NHS review—the broad picture

Patricia Day, Rudolf Klein

"The white paper promises a more flexible organisation capable of adapting to new circumstances. And given the inevitable uncertainties of the future (Who predicted AIDS a decade ago?), its aim should surely be to shape the NHS into a more open, learning organisation where acceptance of change and the ability to cope with it become routine. But if that is indeed Mr Clarke's intention and if it is to be achieved without damaging the patient in the process there will have to be an investment in the change itself—in the new skills and techniques that will be required. If some of the weirder ideas floated in the white paper allow him to gain the Prime Minister's support in extracting the money from the Treasury then their inclusion will have been worth while. And, with a bit of luck, they will never be implemented."

Given the determination of the opposition to present the review of the National Health Service as a revelation of the cloven hoof of Thatcherism, and the government's determination to present it as a millenarian vision, it is all too easy to lose sight of its true importance. Its immediate impact is likely to be less dramatic than expected, apart from the demands on the negotiating time of everyone concerned; its effects over the next decade may, however, be to shift gradually the attitudes and practices of health service providers and consumers alike.

Leaving aside political hyperbole, *Working for Patients* is remarkable for what it does not say.[1] A policy review launched a year ago in an attempt to devise a new funding system has ended up by saying nothing about how to finance the NHS. The government has finally accepted that there is no financial wheeze that can absolve it from responsibility for taking decisions about funding.[2] Such decisions are inescapably political, given that there is no formula for deciding what is right. So the basic principles of the NHS, enshrined in its 1948 settlement, have been reaffirmed; it remains an overwhelmingly tax financed service, universal in its scope and mostly free at the point of use.

But if *Working for Patients* may from one perspective be seen as a preservation order slapped on an ancient monument the workmen are moving in behind the stately façade to remodel the old building. What started out as a review of finance emerged as a review of organisation. But irrespective of the preferences of the government or anyone else it was inevitable that the NHS would have to change.[3] The possibilities created by information technology are transforming managerial systems in public services and private enterprises; there is an international trend for large organisations to break up into smaller units and buy in skills and services from outside. Add to this the semantic revolution that has transformed patients (passive people to whom things are done) into con-

sumers (people actively scrutinising what is on offer)—a transformation mirroring deeper shifts in society—and the inevitability of the NHS having to adapt to a changing environment becomes apparent.

The government appears to have three main objectives: to tighten up the managerial structure in order to ensure central control over the NHS's policies and priorities, to raise efficiency through competition, and to increase consumer choice. Are the proposals likely to achieve the objectives set or do they pull against each other? What needs scrutinising is not the government's emphasis on efficiency and value for money but the appropriateness of the measures proposed: are they feasible, can they be implemented, what will be the cost of so doing (and to whom), and will they yield the expected benefits?

Not surprisingly the clearest proposals are those that deal with the management structure and style of the NHS: their precision is in sharp contrast to the fuzziness of some of the other proposals. This reflects, no doubt, the fact that they build on the logic of the Griffiths managerial revolution. Within the Department of Health there is to be yet another attempt to divorce the political role of setting objectives and the managerial role of implementing policy. Whether relabelling the bodies concerned as the NHS Policy Board and the Management Executive will do the trick remains to be seen. Within the NHS all authorities—regions, districts, and family practitioner committees—are to become explicitly managerial in character: transmission belts for central policy rather than representatives of professional or local interests. Provided that such interests are given other institutionalised means for articulating their views this represents no loss. The contention that a scattering of often press ganged and reluctant local authority nominees is somehow a guarantee of democracy suggests ignorance of either what that concept means, what those nominees actually do, or both.[4]

> "If it is seen as a blueprint of the future, as a firm commitment to specific actions, then there is real cause for scepticism."

Further down the line the proposals imply greater managerial participation in clinical practice. Specifically, managers would participate in defining the terms of consultants' contracts and in setting the criteria for both medical audit and distinction awards. All this could be seen as a threatening breach of the conventions of medical autonomy. Equally, however, it could be argued that the proposals simply implement more fully the logic of what covertly and incompletely has

Centre for the Analysis of Social Policy, University of Bath, Bath BA2 7AY
Patricia Day *research officer*
Rudolf Klein *professor*

3

> *"If, however, it is seen as an indication of the direction in which the NHS will be going over the next decade then it would seem to merit at least two cheers."*

been happening over the last decade or so—that medical practices not only determine the way in which resources are used but also in turn are partly shaped by their availability. Similarly, it is clear that concepts like "quality" have various dimensions and that there are non-medical definitions that have to be accommodated within any audit system. If these arguments carry any conviction then the real test of the review's proposals may lie in the way they are implemented. The result should be to institutionalise greater clinical participation in managerial practice. This assumes, however, an investment in managing change which cannot be taken for granted.

The central paradox of the white paper is that it is trying to develop a stronger managerial framework in order to delegate more freedom. But there is an asymmetry in how much the two sets of proposals have been developed[4]: Mr Clarke has got his bit and bridle, but the horse is still in the stable. Until the Department of Health produces its various supplementary papers it is difficult to come to a definite conclusion about the headline catching proposals for hospitals to opt out of the system and for family practitioner budget holders. Both reflect the influence of Professor Alain Enthoven's advocacy of an internal market to improve efficiency through competition.[5] In both cases everything will turn on the small print. For example, the white paper states that hospitals will be charged the full cost of their capital assets. If so the competitiveness of prices charged by hospitals will depend less on their clinical efficiency than on the way in which their sites and buildings are valued: a factor that may be particularly important in the case of London teaching hospitals with prime inner city sites. Again, in the case of family practitioner budget holders everything would seem to depend on how the government proposes to guard against the possibility of biased selection—that is, concentrating on low risk patients—and whether by the time various safeguards have been introduced there will be much incentive left to take on managerial responsibilities. Certainly the United States experience is not encouraging.[6] And it may be impossible to draw any general conclusions from the experience of a handful of pioneers. By definition they will represent a biased sample of enthusiasts, and even if such natural experiments are rigorously evaluated—as they should be—they may not be generalisable.

Furthermore, competition (whether among hospitals or family practitioners) cannot be equated with consumer choice, as the white paper rather too easily assumes. If a district health authority contracts for services with a particular hospital it will presumably be on price and quality. There will be no consumer choice, although health authorities could write indicators of consumer convenience into the contract: for example, that no patient should have to wait for more than 20 minutes before being seen in outpatients. Similarly, in the case of general practice there is much rhetoric about choice. But choice depends on practitioners competing against each other for customers. Whether increasing the proportion of income derived from capitation fees would bring about that result remains an open question. It is more likely to be brought about by making it easier for doctors to set up

practice where they will; but there are no indications in the white paper of any move towards abolishing existing restrictions, and there is, moreover, an ominous sentence about the government seeking power to limit the total number of practitioners. Similarly, encouraging practices to manage their own budgets may limit choice; the incentives to create large practices may produce geographical monopolies. Lastly, increasing choice may cut across the government's desire to avoid increasing spending. This is particularly true of referrals, where the messages put out by the white paper are somewhat contradictory. It envisages general practitioners being able to refer patients to hospitals where the district has no contract; the health authority would subsequently pick up the bill. If this actually happens then it is difficult to see how district budgets can be controlled.

In interpreting all this, everything turns on how one reads the tone of the white paper. If it is seen as a blueprint of the future, as a firm commitment to

> *"Too often the white paper gives the impression of designing an NHS for acute services, while ignoring the rest."*

specific actions, then there is real cause for scepticism: so much will depend on the fine print of the details, which are not yet available. If, however, it is seen as an indication of the direction in which the NHS will be going over the next decade then it would seem to merit at least two cheers. Some of the proposals are plainly wrong headed: the proposed tax concession for the health insurances of the over 60s sets an expensive precedent and may simply give a bonus to existing policy holders rather than promoting a dramatic growth in their numbers. There is a conspicuous and entirely lamentable failure to give the government's response to the Griffiths report on community care despite the obvious implications for the role of the district health authorities.[7] Too often the white paper gives the impression of designing an NHS for acute services, and particularly elective surgery, while ignoring the rest.

But, more positively, it does seem to set a new style for the NHS. It promises a more flexible organisation —as with wages and salaries—capable of adapting to new circumstances. And given the inevitable uncertainties of the future Who predicted AIDS a decade ago?), the aim should surely be to shape the NHS into a more open, learning organisation where acceptance of change and the ability to cope with it become routine. But if that is indeed Mr Clarke's intention and if it is to be achieved without damaging the patient in the process there will have to be an investment in the change itself—in the new skills and techniques that will be required. If some of the weirder ideas floated in the white paper allow him to gain the Prime Minister's support in extracting the money from the Treasury then their inclusion will have been worthwhile. And, with a bit of luck, they will never be implemented.

1 Secretaries of State for Health, Wales, Northern Ireland, and Scotland. *Working for patients*. London: HMSO, 1989. (Cmnd 555.)
2 Klein R. Financing health care: the three options. *Br Med J* 1988;**296**:734-6.
3 Klein R. Toward a new pluralism. *Health Policy* 1987;**8**:5-12.
4 Day F, Klein R. *Accountabilities*. London: Tavistock, 1987.
5 Enthoven AC. *Reflections on the management of the National Health Service*. London: The Nuffield Provincial Hospitals Trust, 1985.
6 Moore SH, Martin DF, Richardson WC. Does the primary-care gatekeeper control the costs of health care? *New Engl J Med* 1986;**309**:1400-4.
7 Griffiths R. *Community care: agenda for action*. London: HMSO, 1988.

BMA's measured response

Gordon Macpherson *Deputy editor, BMJ*

"The NHS review was born of a financial crisis and has turned out to be as radical as was Aneurin Bevan's 1946 NHS Act. Kenneth Clarke is also a formidable minister who is backed by a Prime Minister with a large parliamentary majority. The profession must formulate its views, remain united, and be prepared for a tough campaign to ensure that the public really does get a better health service and staff better job satisfaction."

The BMA has responded cautiously to the NHS review,[1] not because it has been stunned by ministers' opening sell of their proposals[2] but for three reasons. Firstly, the association's leaders are doubtful that the promise in the white paper's title, *Working for Patients*, will materialise. Secondly, they believe that until the fine print of the forthcoming working papers has been analysed the profession would be unwise to make any policy response. Thirdly, they want the BMA council and the craft committees, which represent all NHS doctors, to give their constituents time to consider the proposals.

This response may seem risky in face of a Secretary of State in a hurry. The timetable for implementing the reforms[3] shows the government's keenness to press ahead. Yet, as members of the Central Committee for Hospital Medical Services warned,[4] that timetable is unrealistic. To impose an election oriented programme on a service that has barely digested its third major restructuring in 15 years and which is still struggling from the nurses' regrading exercise could spell disaster. Furthermore, neither of the two radical proposals —establishing self governing hospitals and introducing budgets for larger general practices—can be achieved without the cooperation of most NHS doctors. So the profession need not let itself be hustled into accepting all or part of the white paper by impatient ministers.

Patricia Day and Rudolf Klein have analysed the white paper's implications in the previous article. The *BMJ* published a summary,[5] highlighted the main proposals,[6] and published an analytical series on the government's plans. The BMA sent a special "white paper" edition of *BMA News Review* to all doctors and it also distributed to all divisions copies of a video programme in which its leaders gave their preliminary assessments. So even doctors who have not seen the white paper will have ample opportunity to assess what *Working for Patients* might mean for the NHS. They should take that opportunity and contribute to local and national meetings that the BMA and its craft committees have planned.[7]

Will the government's promise be fulfilled?

The profession's first concern should be to judge whether the white paper, which offers no extra money for the NHS, will really fulfil the government's promise "to give patients, wherever they live in the UK, better health care and greater choice of the services available. . . ." Despite the government's claim to be preserving the principles of a tax funded health service its novel device of separating funding—which will continue to be mainly tax based—from the provision of services—for which radical ideas are introduced—lays the groundwork for the future dismantling of the NHS. Doctors will have to decide whether the working papers on general practice budgets and on self governing hospitals contain sufficient safeguards to prevent a two tier service developing. The dilemma will then be whether the necessary safeguards will not so restrict the two ventures as to nullify any worth they may have in offering a more flexible and independent use of resources. That dilemma might have been resolved without subjecting the whole service to upheaval if the government had accepted the advice of the BMA, Alain Enthoven, and others to try any new ideas out in pilot schemes.[8][9] The Secretary of State has rejected such an approach, which is odd given that the two radical proposals will be introduced only if hospitals and practices volunteer to take part. Doctors might be more willing to participate if there was evidence to show that the reforms produced better care for patients.

Ministers have not even waited for an evaluation of the six resource management initiatives due towards the end of this year.[10] The outcomes of these initiatives are crucial to the operation of general practice budgets and of self governing hospitals. Without accurate up to date information the new system will work no better than the existing one. Consultants at the CCHMS meeting last week were sceptical about the intention "during 1989, to extend preparation for the resource management initiative in up to 50 acute hospitals . . . with the aim of building up coverage to 260 acute units by the end of 1991-2." Several described the objectives as belonging to cloud cuckoo land.

"The profession's first concern should be to judge whether the white paper will really fulfil the government's promise."

Collecting and using information have long been great weaknesses in the NHS. The government proposes to spend £40m on information technology, but many think that much more than that figure may be needed. The encouragement of medical audit and the plans to monitor health authorities and family practitioner committees are to be welcomed. But these improvements together with the improvements in information might well have been enough to improve the service without resorting to untried plans for general practitioner budgets and the opting out of hospitals.

One of the Secretary of State's innovations, the information cascade for staff, suggests that he was anxious to get his message across before their own organisations had a chance to waylay his plans. That objective was jeopardised by the Labour party's leaked version of the white paper. This and earlier leaks gave the BMA a pointer to refining the next stage of its parliamentary and public relations campaign on the review.[8 11] Although doctors may not like it, the fate of this white paper could turn as much on the skills of public relations experts as on the arguments of medical experts. That ministers are wary of the BMA is suggested by remarks accusing it of a "dithering" response to the proposals and for never having been in favour "of any change of any kind on any subject for as long as anyone can remember...." To anyone familiar with the BMA such hyperbole should be filed under that Whitehall heading "being economical with the truth."

Some of the proposed reforms—for example, medical audit and more effective prescribing—will be supported by the public and by many doctors, and these and the more contentious ideas such as stricter monitoring of doctors' working patterns will be discussed by the profession's representatives and health ministers. For general practitioners, however, any discussions will be overshadowed by a year of little progress in negotiations on the white paper on primary care. The General Medical Services Committee's negotiators were angry that the Department of Health had continued these discussions when it must have known that they would be overtaken by the white paper.[12] The committee met on 16 February to approve a paper setting out the history of the negotiations as well as the implications of *Working for Patients* for general practice. It was sent to all practitioners to help them and their representatives prepare for the special conference of local medical committees on 27 April.

Doctors set to lose their influence

Local medical committees might lose much of their influence in primary care if the new family practitioner committees answerable to regional health authorities are set up. Indeed, the whole profession looks set to lose much of its influence in a service that will be run by management boards stripped of any local or staff representation. This change, the threat to the Whitley council's negotiating machinery, more local flexibility in pay, and freedom for self governing hospitals to negotiate their own terms and conditions of service all accord with the government's policies of greater competition and limited union power. They also have implications for the future of the review bodies, the career prospects of hospital staff, and the even spread of good quality hospital services throughout the country, which is a notable success of the NHS.

This review, which was born of a financial crisis, has turned out to be as radical as was Aneurin Bevan's 1946 NHS Act. Kenneth Clarke is also a formidable minister who is backed by a Prime Minister with a large parliamentary majority. The profession must formulate its views, remain united, and be prepared for a tough campaign to ensure that the public really does get a better health service and staff better job satisfaction.

1 Secretaries of State for Health, Wales, Northern Ireland and Scotland. *Working for patients.* London: HMSO, 1989. (Cmnd 555.)
2 Delamothe T. Review review. *Br Med J* 1989;**298**:394.
3 Beecham L. NHS review: government's timetable. *Br Med J* 1989;**298**:392.
4 Beecham L. Patient's choice at risk, warn consultants. *Br Med J* 1989;**298**: 390-2.
5 Warden J. NHS review. *Br Med J* 1989;**298**:275.
6 Beecham L. NHS review: main proposals in white paper. *Br Med J* 1989;**298**:390.
7 Beecham L. BMA's provisional timetable. *Br Med J* 1989;**298**:392.
8 British Medical Association. Evidence to the government internal review of the National Health Service. *Br Med J* 1988;**296**:1411-8.
9 Enthoven AC. *Reflections on the management of the National Health Service.* London: Nuffield Provincial Hospitals Trust, 1985.
10 Beecham L. Consultants urged to take part in resource management. *Br Med J* 1988;**296**:511.
11 Anonymous. BMA checklist for government's NHS review. *Br Med J* 1989;**298**:124.
12 Beecham L. LMC's call to stop white paper talks rejected. *Br Med J* 1989;**298**:53.

New health care market

Ray Robinson

The white paper's proposals provide an incentive for improving and diffusing efficiency throughout the National Health Service. In particular, charging health authorities for their capital assets and new investments will ensure that these are used to the full, and more patient choice may result from general practitioner budget holders purchasing hospital services directly. But much will depend on how the plans are implemented—will providing long term care, for the mentally ill or the chronically sick, for example, be an attractive source of revenue, and will less mobile patients be penalised?

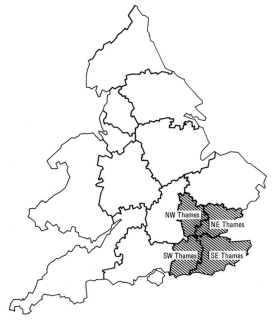

With capital charging hospitals in the expensive south east may find it hard to compete

The belief that a competitive environment stimulates efficiency and enhances consumer choice has been a central component of the government's economic strategy for the past 10 years. With the publication of the white paper *Working For Patients* its plans for extending this approach to the NHS have finally been unwrapped.[1] A key component of this strategy will be competition between short stay hospitals for service contracts from district health authorities acting as purchasing agents, from general practitioner budget holders, and from private patients and insurance plans.

The origin of these ideas lies in the work of the American health economist, Alain Enthoven.[2] During a visit to Britain in 1985 he noted that the NHS commanded widespread support but that it provided few incentives for efficiency. As a result wide variations in performance exist between hospitals and districts. These include differences in operating theatre utilisation, levels of bed use, and the extent to which clinical staff make productive use of their time. His suggested remedy was to retain those features that make the NHS such a popular institution—especially universal access within a tax financed, free at point of use system—but to improve efficiency through trade in clinical services between district health authorities. This arrangement has become known as an internal market.

The white paper builds on this model but goes a good deal further. The rudiments of its proposal for a new health care market in hospital services are shown in the figure.

The government's plans envisage separation of responsibility for the purchase of services from their delivery. Three main types of budget holders will be included in the purchasing arrangements. Existing district health authorities will act as purchasing agents for most of the inpatient care received by their resident population. Where these services are provided will be determined by district managers in consultation with referring general practitioners. In addition, however, general practitioners with list sizes of over 11 000 patients will be given the opportunity to become direct budget holders for selected hospital services. Services they will be able to purchase directly on behalf of their patients include diagnostic tests, outpatient services, and a defined group of inpatient and day cases, such as hip replacements and cataract removals. As with districts, general practices which opt to be budget holders will be free to purchase these services from hospitals of their choosing. Finally, private patients and insurance plans may be expected to figure increasingly as purchasers of services.

On the supply side services will be provided by hospitals that continue to be managed directly by the district health authority, by private hospitals, and by a new category of self governing hospitals acting as independent trusts within the public sector. Self governing hospitals play a key part in the government's plans for the future. Initially, major short stay hospitals with more than 250 beds have been identified as suitable candidates for self governing status, but eventually other hospitals may be eligible.

The rationale underlying the new health care market is that competition provides both an incentive structure for improving efficiency and a transmission mechanism for spreading it throughout the service. Hospitals which can provide high quality, cost effective services will be able to obtain funds for expanding workloads and this will act as a spur to less efficient ones. This contrasts with existing financial arrangements in which cash limits often penalise efficiency by restricting a hospital's ability to use its capacity to the full.

Whether or not these expected advantages materialise will depend crucially on the way in which the proposals are implemented. The white paper provides a blueprint not a working model. It leaves many

King's Fund Institute, London NW1 7NF
Ray Robinson, MSCECON, *health policy analyst*

Br Med J 1989;**298**:437-9

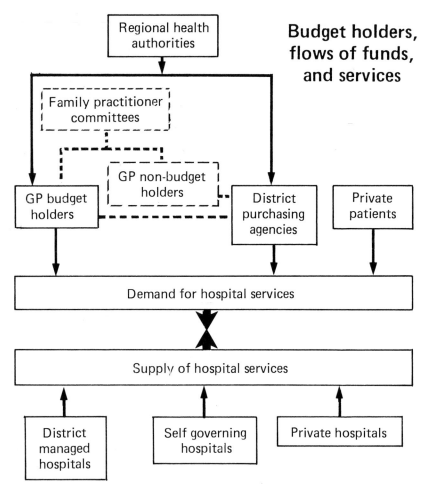

Budget holders, flows of funds, and services

Regional health authorities → **Family practitioner committees** (dashed box) → **GP budget holders**, **GP non-budget holders** (dashed box), **District purchasing agencies**, **Private patients**

→ **Demand for hospital services** ⨯ **Supply of hospital services**

← **District managed hospitals**, **Self governing hospitals**, **Private hospitals**

New health care markets for hospital services: budget holders, flows of funds, and services

questions unanswered, particularly about competition.
- How far will competition be allowed to develop?
- Will competition increase consumer choice?
- Will it be possible to link management's objectives with the activities of clinicians?
- Will competition jeopardise the aim of universal access to health care?

Competition, prices, and regulation

For competition to produce an efficient allocation of resources certain conditions have to be met. At the most fundamental level prices need to reflect the real cost of providing services. Otherwise market "signals" will be distorted. This requirement makes the government's decision to introduce a system of capital charges into the NHS a sensible one. As the white paper points out capital assets are at present often treated as a costless "free good." There is little incentive to ensure that they are employed to the full. From April 1991, however, health authorities will be charged for their existing capital assets and new investments.

But if hospitals begin to charge for capital assets, including rental payments that reflect the current value of their sites, it might lead to some unexpected developments. Most notably, it would provide a powerful incentive for the relocation of some services away from high value, inner city sites, especially in London. Herein lies a tension. The need to ensure that certain core services are always made available locally will mean that the government will be unwilling to allow market processes totally to determine location decisions. The new resource allocation formula addresses this problem by taking account of the relative costs of providing services in different areas. The Thames regions, for example, will receive larger capitation payments than elsewhere. While it is quite

proper for the government to modify economic forces to pursue social objectives, such intervention does raise the question of the size of the efficiency loss that it is prepared to incur to meet this aim.

Limits placed on the size of capital programmes may also be a source of inefficiency: borrowing restraints will continue to limit managers' freedom to determine the optimal size of their investment programmes. District managed hospitals will still have their investment

---

"The white paper provides a blueprint not a working model. It leaves many questions unanswered, particularly about competition."

---

funds allocated by regions within an overall programme total. Self governing hospitals will face an annual financing limit set each year by the Secretary of State as part of the public expenditure planning process. The fear must be that an undercapitalised service will still be restricted by a public expenditure policy which owes more to macroeconomic objectives than to the needs of the health service. Private hospitals, of course, will not be similarly constrained.

An important feature of a competitive market is that firms should be free to expand and contract. New firms appear and successful firms expand, while unsuccessful firms contract and sometimes go out of business. But this could be an expensive process for the NHS. New investment would be required in those hospitals gaining patients while excess capacity existed elsewhere. Unlike the successful private firm, which does not have to bear the costs of its rivals' unused capacity, it would clearly be wasteful for the NHS to add to capacity at some hospitals while it was left idle elsewhere.

Consumer choice

More patient choice is a theme that runs throughout the white paper. Markets are an established mechanism for providing choice. How far will the new health care market meet this aim? There should be more diversity in the supply of services, with general practitioners acting as budget holders. The removal of obstacles to changing a general practitioner will also enhance the patients' choice. General practitioner budget holders who purchase hospital services directly on behalf of their patients will have more choice. Better information systems should enable general practitioners to select hospitals where waiting times are shorter. All these changes offer genuine scope for greater responsiveness to patients' preferences. For core hospital services, however, the impact of the white paper's proposals is less clear.

Districts as purchasing agencies will be responsible for determining where service contracts are placed. The white paper states that they will need to "take account of" general practitioners' existing referral patterns and "discuss...the possibility of changing those patterns." Without knowledge of existing referral patterns it is impossible to say how much change will be necessary. But the need to ensure that referrals are consistent with district service contracts is clearly a potential source of restriction on general practitioners' existing freedom of referral. At the very least this will require some extremely delicate negotiations.

In a free market managers set their firm's objectives in terms of profitability, sales revenue, growth targets, and other financial variables. It is competition between rival firms pursuing similar objectives that produces an efficient allocation of resources. The division of responsibilities within a hospital makes it far less easy to ensure that everyone works towards a common objective.[3] The link between the management's financial objectives and the activities of clinicians is particularly problematic.

Managing clinical activity

The white paper proposes the delegation of more authority to hospital managers. They will be responsible for gaining service contracts from purchasers by offering cost effective services that patients actually want. Their funding will depend on their success in attracting business. But while managers will have overall responsibility for financial performance consultants will continue to make clinical decisions that determine the way money is actually spent. They will also have the ultimate responsibility for meeting any changes in workloads—upwards or downwards—resulting from service contracts.

It has, of course, been the recognition of the clinician's pivotal role in committing expenditure that has led to successive attempts to persuade them to participate formally in decisions about the use of resources. The resource management initiative is the latest attempt to encourage further participation of doctors and nurses in management. The government intends to extend the resource management initiative to 20 short stay hospital sites by the end of 1989, with

Much of the time of those caring for the elderly is spent in liaising between hospitals, social services, and community services. The white paper provides no evidence that this job will become any easier

the aim of building up to 260 units by the end of 1991-2. Is this ambitious timetable feasible?

Despite the considerable enthusiasm displayed by some of the participants at the resource management sites, one recent research study concluded that general experience of including clinicians in budgetary decisions was disappointing: neither managers nor doctors have shown much enthusiasm.[4] This does not augur well for plans to extend the initiative nation wide over such a short period, especially as the additional complication of workload funding will be added to the existing difficulties with which the initiative is having to grapple. Moreover, it is also of concern that the decision to extend the initiative has been taken before the Department of Health's evaluation of it—by a team at Brunel University—has been completed. The final report is not due until towards the end of 1989.

Access to health care

While competition may yield efficiency gains there is always a danger that without safeguards these will be achieved at the expense of a loss of equity.

Services offering clear revenue earning potential will become more attractive. Many health promotion and screening services—primarily aimed at the affluent, worried well—are likely to fall into this category. Similarly, it will be easy to draw up service contracts for well defined, short stay, minor elective surgery. Providing long term care for the mentally ill and handicapped, the chronically sick, or for elderly people suffering from dementia may hold less attraction as a source of revenue.

Access to services will also be influenced by the

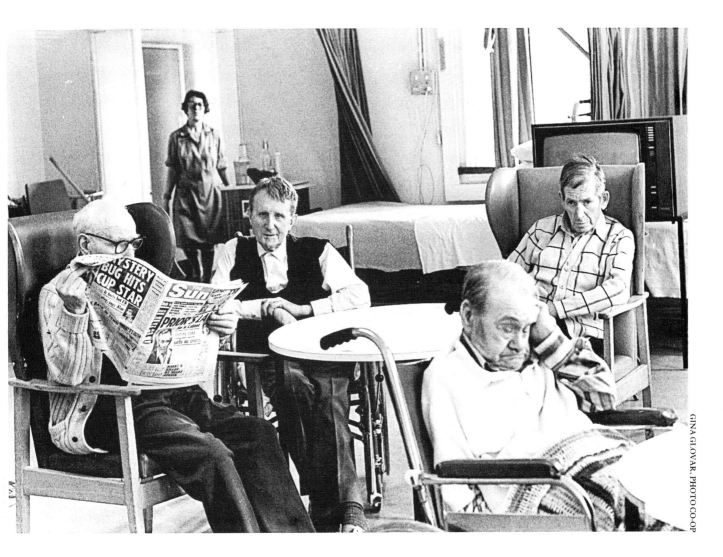

9

location of services resulting from the competitive process. If competition leads to greater specialisation and the concentration of services at fewer sites there will be greater need for some patients to travel further for treatment. This might penalise less mobile people and their families. Continuity of care after hospital discharge for those patients treated outside their home districts may also be a problem. Liaison between hospitals and local general practitioners, social service departments, and community services is already a cause of concern. Treatment at a distance might exacerbate these difficulties.

The white paper is a tantalising document. It offers the prospect for major improvements in the way that health finances are used and services delivered. It specifies the broad strategies of decentralisation and competition that the government believes will bring about these improvements. But there are many pitfalls. Much will depend on the way that the strategy is implemented. In particular, potential conflicts among the pursuit of cost efficiency, equity, and the quality of care will require careful attention.

1 Secretaries of State for Health, Wales, Northern Ireland, and Scotland. *Working for patients*. London: HMSO, 1989. (Cmnd 555.)
2 Enthoven AC. *Reflections on the management of the National Health Service*. London: Nuffield Provincial Hospitals Trust, 1985.
3 McGuire A, Henderson J, Mooney G. *The economics of health care*. London: Routledge and Kegan Paul, 1988.
4 Pollitt C, Harrison S, Hunter D, Marnoch G. The reluctant managers: clinicians and budgets in the NHS. *Finance Accountability and Management* 1988;**213**:33.

What will competition provide for these consumers? Better, more flexible care, or will they be spurned by their local self governing hospital in favour of an easier source of revenue?

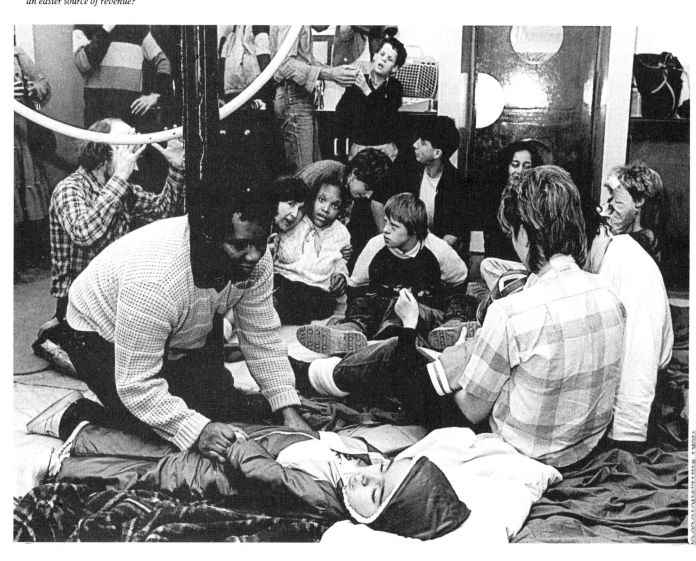

Streamlining management

Alan Bussey

There are two major themes in the changed management patterns proposed for the NHS: separation of commissioning or buying health services from providing them and an emphasis on the management role of the health authorities. Although these structural changes will end some confusion, the altered, smaller, membership will also lose the invaluable link between the local authority services as well as the first hand experience of the professional members. There will remain several possible forms of medical input to health authorities: executive membership, appointing the director of public health as an executive, a strengthened medical advisory machinery, and the local community health council. Finally, will smaller districts merge with one another and with family practitioner committees—and, if this is widespread what then will be the role of regional health authorities?

Lewisham and North Southwark Health Authority, London SE1 9RY
Alan Bussey, FFCM, specialist in community medicine

Br Med J 1989;298:512-3

The proposals in the white paper *Working for Patients* have been described as "the most far-reaching reform of the National Health Service in its forty year history."[1] No one reading its hundred pages could disagree. Of the seven key measures proposed, those concerned with the governance of the NHS are as radical as any. There are differences of detail in the proposals for Scotland, Wales, and Northern Ireland but the principles are identical with those described here for England.

At the top level in England a new NHS policy board, chaired and appointed by the Secretary of State, will determine the strategy, objectives, and finances of the NHS. This board will also oversee the next level—the NHS management executive, which will deal with all operational matters in the NHS (including, for the first time, family practitioner committees) and will be led by a chief executive.

This structure is similar to that proposed in the first Griffiths report but never fully implemented.[2] The new arrangements should be welcomed for removing the confusion between policy setting and management that led to the present NHS Management Board being chaired successively by the first chief executive, ministers of state, and, latterly, the Secretary of State—to the bewilderment of the rest of the NHS.

At the next level down regional health authorities are to remain but are to concentrate on setting performance criteria for and monitoring the performance of those below them and evaluating the effectiveness of the NHS. They will shed many of the support services that can better be provided by district health authorities, agencies, or the private sector. The legal, information, building, and works bureaucracies of regional health authorities are among those that will lose their monopoly position and will have to compete or die. The remit of regional health authorities will be extended to embrace family practitioner committees as well as district health authorities—bringing together for the first time at a strategic level the main arms of the NHS.

Delegation to units

District health authorities are similarly to be slimmed by further delegation to units—particularly to major hospitals. In the words of the white paper "like regional health authorities, district health authorities can then concentrate on ensuring that the health needs of the population for which they are responsible are met; that there are effective services for the prevention and control of diseases and the promotion of health; and that their population has access to a comprehensive range of high quality, value-for-money services."

The governance of both regional health authorities and district health authorities will be changed dramatically by fusing the management team with an authority whose membership is reduced in size. The new authorities will be composed of five non-executive members, up to five executive members (managers), and a non-executive chairman. Membership places reserved for local authority, trade unions, medical, and nursing nominees are swept away with the sole exception of a medical school representative on authorities in teaching districts.

As well as losing their direct link with the Department of Health family practitioner committees are to be reduced in size in line with other authorities from 30 members to 11. There will be five lay members and four professionals (instead of the present 15) including one doctor in general practice. Together with the chairman, the committee will appoint the eleventh member—the chief executive. This post will carry wider responsibilities and scope than do present family practitioner committee administrators. Consequently, salaries will be higher and the posts will be open to competition from managers inside and outside the NHS.

Finally, a new kind of management authority is to be created in the self governing hospitals. These hospitals will have a substantial degree of independence within the NHS and each will be run by an NHS hospital trust. Their boards of directors will have no more than 11 members (including the chairman) with a balanced number of executive and non-executive directors. Two of the latter will be drawn from the local community associated with the hospital; employees of the NHS are barred. The executive directors, however, will include a medical director and a senior nurse manager in addition to the finance director and the general manager. To be permitted to achieve self governing status hospitals must show that they are well managed at present and senior professional staff, especially consultants, must be concerned in the management of the hospital.

Two important themes run through these organisational changes. The first begins the separation of the commissioning or buying of health services from their provision. The second takes further the managerial revolution in the NHS by slimming health authorities and tailoring them more closely to a management role, thereby ending all pretence to a representative function. As part of this aim consultants are to be given greater opportunities to manage hospitals and their services, but the medical presence on authorities above hospital level, as of right, is lost.

Ending a period of confusion

Whatever views may be expressed for or against this approach the removal of the representative element will end a long period of confuison. There is no doubt that many district health authority members, for example, have found it difficult to see a clear role for themselves since the introduction of general management. This dilemma has been particularly acute for generalist members when decisions on closures or reductions in service have been required. Many have been torn between their concern for the effects on the population for which they feel

Sir Roy Griffith in 1983: "A small strong general management body is necessary at the centre to ensure that responsibility is pushed as far down the line as possible."

responsible and their corporate management responsibility.

The problem has been different for local authority members. Their contributions and reactions to unpleasant decisions have often been frankly political, reflecting the views of their particular party in an almost reflex way. It seems likely that this partisan approach by some local authority members has contributed to their exclusion from the new arrangements.

While this exclusion may help the new authorities to focus on the tasks of management by removing the representational distraction, there will be losses too. In several health authorities the local authority members have provided an invaluable link with the social services, education, environmental health, and housing committees of their authorities. These services are key partners in many health authority plans and initiatives, and the more thoughtful and less strident

local authority members have often been able to oil the committee and financial wheels to make things happen. It may be that the long delayed government response to the Griffiths report on community care will provide alternative mechanisms.[3] It is difficult to see, however, any alternative that will adequately replace the intimate knowledge which many local authority members now have of the strategies and plans of both sides.

A third group of members of present authorities are the professionals—the consultant, general practitioner, and nurse members. Appointed for their personal qualities rather than as lobbyists for their professional constituencies, they have contributed a skill that has illuminated many debates and has been valued by lay members and chairmen alike. They have often been torn in the same way as have the generalist members but with the added burden of their knowledge of the aims, pressures, and frustrations of medicine and nursing in the NHS. The white paper's proposals seem to rule out this kind of contribution in future because no place is reserved for doctors in the non-executive membership of the new health authorities, save for the lone general practitioner on the family practitioner committee. The profession will no doubt wish to explore in discussions with the government whether doctors are to be appointed non-executive members of health authorities "on the basis of the skills and experience they can bring to the authority," to quote the white paper.

Medical input to health authorities

If they are not other areas become crucially important to the profession in terms of medical input to health authorities. Perhaps the most important is executive membership, where there are several possible ways to include doctors. Five executive members (managers) are proposed for regional health authorities and district health authorities with places already identified for the finance director and general manager. Few districts have a medically qualified district general manager but more have doctors managing large units. So the opportunity exists in many district health authorities for management arrangements to be made to enable clinician managers to become executive members of authorities (at least until their hospitals become NHS hospital trusts) in the same way as the white paper describes how clinicians can become executive directors on the boards of self governing hospitals.

A second route to member level flows from the new emphasis on the responsibilities of authorities to ensure that the health needs of their population are met; that there are effective services for the prevention and control of diseases and the promotion of health; and that their population has access to a comprehensive range of high quality, value for money services. To discharge these functions it will be essential for the regional health authority or district health authority to appoint its director of public health (on whose annual report on the health of the population many of the authority's decisions will be based) as an executive director.

Another important avenue for medical input to management is, of course, the medical advisory machinery of regional health authorities, district health authorities, and family practitioner committees. This will assume much greater importance to the profession and I hope to the health authorities as well. In many districts and some regions and family practitioner committee areas this will require an overhaul of the profession's machinery and improvement in the content and quality of discussions if authorities are to take any notice.

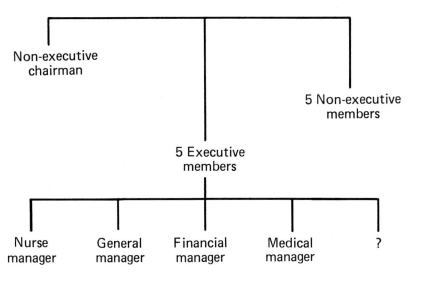

Lost — membership places reserved for local authority, trade union, medical, and nursing nominees

Proposed governance of health authorities

A third, albeit more remote, route for medical input will be the local community health council. The removal of the last vestige of the consumer role of health authorities leaves this way clear for community health councils. The profile of many of them will be raised, not least because local authorities excluded from health authority membership in future will see community health councils as a natural platform for political or non-political debates about health. In consequence, some community health councils may be hijacked by local authorities, but all should see the quality of their membership, information, and debates improved. In these circumstances the profession locally would do well to consider closer links with community health councils.

> ## *"In a changing landscape there is one certainty . . . that the structural reforms will occur."*

In a changing landscape there is one certainty and several possibilities. That certainty is that the structural reforms will occur. No working papers or debates seem to be contemplated on this part of the white paper. So, by April 1991, restructured regional health authorities, district health authorities, and family practitioner committees will be in place together with an unknown number of NHS hospital trusts.

Turning to possibilities, if implementation continues beyond the next general election more and more district health authorities will lose their acute hospitals and perhaps other services. They will turn their attention from direct management of the provision of care to analysing the needs of their populations, planning and purchasing packages of services to meet those needs, and evaluating the results in terms of quality and outcome. Many district populations are too small to carry out these functions efficiently or effectively. Moreover, there are insufficient numbers of people with skills in these areas to cover 200 authorities. Mergers of districts with each other and with family practitioner committees as foreshadowed in the white paper are likely to follow. If as a result of this the number of authorities is reduced to, say, 50 or 60 questions will then arise about the continuing roles of regional health authorities, which, by then, would have only three or four authorities below each of them.

But the real joker in the restructuring pack is the proposal for general practitioners to hold budgets and contract for services. If this initiative prospers and most general practitioners take on these responsibilities and become skilled at them they will resemble health maintenance organisations on the American model more and more. General practitioners and their teams will then be providing preventive and primary care, buying secondary care from hospitals, and then providing aftercare back in the community. If there is a role for health authorities at any level it is likely to be reduced to financial allocation and perhaps the monitoring of quality and outcome.

When considering all these possibilities doctors, managers, and patients alike may perhaps be forgiven for echoing Sam Weller in *The Pickwick Papers* when he said, "in which case it gets too excitin' to be pleasant."

1 Secretaries of State for Health, Wales, Northern Ireland; and Scotland. *Working for patients.* London: HMSO, 1989. (Cmnd 555.)
2 NHS Management Inquiry. *Report.* London: DHSS, 1983. (Griffiths report.)
3 Griffiths R. *Community care: agenda for action.* London: HMSO, 1988.

Information please—and quick

Nick Black

Developing information systems to produce high quality data is daunting—and almost certainly impossible on the proposed timescale. So far systems have been designed by information scientists and imposed from the centre, and there is little sign of a radical change in approach. The difficulties encountered in the six resource management pilot sites make it improbable that 20 acute hospital units will be ready by the end of 1989—let alone 260 by March 1992. The task should be assessed more realistically.

Only one of the government's five aims for the reorganisation of the NHS seems likely to meet with universal support—the need to improve the information available about health services.[1] From the government's point of view it is also the most important in that all the main proposals depend for their success on the ready availability of appropriate, complete, valid, and timely data. While the information requirements of medical audit and resource management are obvious, other proposals are equally dependent on prompt, reliable facts. If district health authorities, general practitioners, and the public are to make informed choices when selecting service providers they will need high quality data not only on costs and waiting times but also on outcomes. And this requirement applies not just to NHS facilities but also to the private sector—and major health insurance companies are already starting to undertake this. In addition, improved information will be needed to enable managers, both in NHS and trust hospitals, to monitor whether consultants are fulfilling their newly agreed contractual obligations. Developing and introducing the necessary information systems is a daunting prospect. To achieve such a task on the timescale envisaged in the white paper is almost certainly impossible. This is largely because so little progress has been made in the past, particularly in the development of clinical information.

Poor quality of information

Clinicians and health services researchers have long recognised the poor quality of information on clinical activity in NHS hospitals. Apart from published reports showing inaccuracies in hospital activity analysis data,[2-4] almost all clinicians have their own examples of incomplete and erroneous information. The resulting lack of credibility of the data—despite the massive effort by clinicians, coding clerks, information officers, and managers in creating, collecting, and processing them—means that little use is made of the product. The replacement of hospital activity analyses with the hospital episode system seems unlikely to be any better. Given the good intention of those who set up and maintain the original system, why has the result been so disappointing? The principal reason is that as with other NHS initiatives the hospital activity analysis was devised as part of an information technology strategy which had as its key feature the centralisation of data for administrative purposes. Instead of starting with an information strategy based on the needs of those who directly provided health care, systems were designed by information technologists and imposed from the centre. While the limitations of having to use large mainframe computers contributed to such decisions in the past, the development of cheap powerful microcomputers has removed this constraint. Despite such technical advances there are as yet few signs in the NHS of the radical change in approach to clinical information systems that is so urgently required.

The key to a new approach is the development of an information (rather than information technology) strategy that is based on a consideration of why clinical information is required. The three principal reasons are confirmed in the white paper. These are

● To enable clinicians to improve the quality of patient care by means of clinical audit as almost all methods of quality assurance require a reliable database
● To improve the running of local services by providing information for resource management or other schemes that combine clinical and financial data, soon to be an essential requirement
● To provide information to the public and parliament to whom the NHS is accountable.

If an accurate database is established for the first of these tasks information can be extracted from it for the second task, which in turn can provide the necessary data for the third task.

Such an approach based on networks of dispersed microcomputers, in which each one is dedicated to a particular activity, raises several questions. What information is needed and wanted by clinicians and managers? What level of detail is required? For example, would a three digit diagnostic code rather than the current four digit code be sufficient for routine data? What clinical information needs to be collected routinely on every patient and what would be more appropriate for occasional ad hoc collection? If dispersed microcomputers are used who will be responsible for the accuracy of the information? And how will confidentiality of clinical data be maintained?

Some health authorities and boards had already recognised the need to adopt a new approach before the publication of the white paper and had started to install information systems based on the requirements of local data users. For example, in the North West Thames Regional Health Authority a standard obstetric information system has been developed and installed in all the main maternity units. This provides data for obstetricians and midwives to audit the work of their own unit. The district, regional, and national data requirements established by the Körner working parties can be met from the same database.[5] Standard

Department of Public Health and Policy, London School of Hygiene and Tropical Medicine, London WC1E 7HT
Nick Black, MD, *senior lecturer in health services research*

Br Med J 1989;298:586-7

systems are extending this strategy into other key areas of the hospital.

Improbable timetable

Despite these developments and those in other parts of the country an immense amount of work remains to be done. The white paper recognises this when it identifies two particular problems: the need for improvements in the coding of medical records and the development of case mix groups. Recognition of the first of these is ironic given the current difficulties and confusion caused by the recent introduction of the new operative procedure codes by the Office of Population Censuses and Surveys.[7-9] Such technical problems can of course be overcome if sufficient resources are applied to seeking solutions. What is less certain is the ability of the NHS to introduce change as rapidly as the government plans. The difficulties encountered over the past few years in the six resource management pilot sites makes it improbable that 20 acute hospital units will be ready by the end of this year, let alone 260 units by March 1992. Not only are such developments likely to cost around £1 billion but they would also require a commitment to training and supporting clinicians and managers throughout the country. These are not arguments against the improvement of information and the introduction of resource management but a plea for a more realistic estimation of the task that lies ahead. Like many if not all government pronouncements, the NHS white paper is probably as much rhetoric as it is a detailed prescription. If so, and if it leads to major benefits as regards the quality of clinical information it will in that regard at least have made a useful contribution to improving health care in Britain.

BMA NEWS REVIEW

Information at her fingertips— but not yet

microcomputer based systems are being provided for all the surgical specialties to enable surgeons to monitor and audit their inpatient work. In view of the differing case mix among surgeons within the same hospital it has been necessary to establish a mechanism for comparative audit across the region, an activity being facilitated by a regional audit group along similar lines to that in Lothian.[6] Developments in operating theatre systems, which will enable anaesthetic audit to be undertaken, and accident and emergency department

1 Secretaries of State for Health, Wales, Northern Ireland, and Scotland. *Working for patients.* London: HMSO, 1989.
2 Whates PD, Birzgalis AR, Irving M. Accuracy of hospital activity analysis codes. *Br Med J* 1982;**284**:1857-8.
3 Buck N, Devlin HB, Lunn JN. *The report of a confidential enquiry into perioperative deaths.* London: Nuffield Provincial Hospital Trust/The King's Fund, 1987.
4 Skinner PW, Riley D, Thomas EM. Use and abuse of performance indicators. *Br Med J* 1988;**297**:1256-9.
5 Health Services Information Steering Group. *A report on the collection and use of information about clinical activity in the NHS.* London: HMSO, 1982.
6 Gruer R, Gordon DS, Gunn AA, Ruckley CV. Audit of surgical audit. *Lancet* 1986;i:23-6.
7 Office of Population Censuses and Surveys. *Classification of surgical operations and procedures.* 4th revision. London: OPCS, 1987.
8 Earlam R. Körner, nomenclature, and SNOMED. *Br Med J* 1988;**296**:903-5.
9 Ellis B. Körner, nomenclature, and SNOMED. *Br Med J* 1988;**296**:1261.

Consumerism and general practice

Ralph Leavey, David Wilkin, David H H Metcalfe

The new consumerism relies on patients being willing and able to choose their general practitioners in the same way as they choose goods and services. But not only does geography limit the available choice of general practitioners, other constraints are also imposed by general practitioners, such as practice boundaries and ceilings on list sizes. Moreover, only 5% of patients change doctors because they are dissatisfied. Thus any move to increase consumer choice in Britain will face considerable inertia and it is unlikely dramatically to improve the quality of general practitioner care.

Centre for Primary Care Research, Department of General Practice, University of Manchester, Manchester M14 5NP

Ralph Leavey, MPHIL, *research fellow*
David Wilkin, PHD, *associate director*
David H H Metcalfe, FRCGP, *professor*

Correspondence to: Mr R Leavey, Centre for Primary Care Research, Department of General Practice, University of Manchester, Rusholme Health Centre, Walmer Street, Manchester M14 5NP.

Br Med J 1989;298:737-9

In the current political and economic climate market forces reign supreme when it comes to regulating the quantity and quality of goods and services. The NHS is no exception to the government's determination to foster competition and enhance the power of the consumer. The white paper *Working for Patients* recommends ways of using the power of the market to improve health services.[1]

The review aims to attach a clearer monetary value to patients by making capitation a much larger element of general practitioner remuneration and through the proposed budget scheme for large practices. Practices and hospitals "which attract the most custom will receive the most money." Thus, "both general practitioners and hospitals will have a real incentive to put patients first." In the interests of providing a better service "general practitioners will be encouraged to compete for patients." To achieve this "it will be easier for patients to choose (and change) their own general practitioner as they wish." The strategy rests on patients making decisions about their doctor in comparison with others.

Before embracing the new consumerism in health care with unqualified enthusiasm it is advisable to examine the premises on which its success will depend. It relies on patients (consumers) being willing and able to exercise choices about their doctors in the same way as they do about restaurants, hairdressers, or supermarkets. In order for the market mechanism to work consumers need to possess the motivation to exercise choice, a range of alternatives from which to choose, information about those alternatives, the competence to make a rational choice, and the opportunity to implement their choice once it has been made. Although the white paper repeatedly asserts the importance which ministers attach to greater consumer choice, it contains no analysis of the extent to which these conditions are currently met.

Motivation to exercise choice

Most people change their doctor only when circumstances force them to do so, either because they have moved or because their general practitioner has retired, moved, or died. Only 5% change doctors because they are dissatisfied with the treatment or attitude of their existing doctor.[2] Perhaps more importantly from the point of view of motivation is the finding that only one in 10 people even think about changing their doctor.[2 4] The vast majority are, rightly or wrongly, satisfied with their present doctor.

The reasons for this lack of motivation to consider alternatives are not hard to find. The nature of people's need for the services of general practitioners and the circumstances in which it arises do little to motivate them to embark on a search for a better doctor. For many their need for medical care is spasmodic and minimal. If contact with the doctor is limited to 10 minutes a year for a prescription for a cough or cold why spend much time thinking about alternatives? When an urgent need does arise because of a serious illness the very fact that it requires urgent treatment precludes the possibility of shopping around. For patients suffering from chronic conditions the reasons for inertia are different but no less powerful. The doctor has become an important part of their lives. The relationship of trust and confidence which has been established during the course of the illness provides a powerful motivation to stay put.

Nevertheless, some patients are dissatisfied and it is possible that more would consider a change if they were aware of alternatives. The College of Health has suggested that there are patients who wish to change their doctors but who believe that to make such a move is difficult and that it would mark them as someone who is "a problem."[5]

Range of accessible alternatives

The notion of consumer choice can be meaningful only if there is a range of alternatives from which to choose. Although there are 30 000 general practitioners in the United Kingdom, various factors combine to

> *". . . the proposals advanced by ministers owe more to political ideology and rhetoric."*

limit the choice available to most people to perhaps three or four practices, and for many of those living in rural areas to only one practice. The simple geographical distribution of doctors places important constraints on the potential effects of any attempt to create a more competitive environment.[6]

On top of the basic geographical constraints are a series of additional factors that further restrict the range of choices practically available. Constraints imposed by general practitioners include the drawing of practice boundaries, unwillingness to accept patients leaving another practice, ceilings on list size,

Changing their GP? Only one in 10 even think of doing so now

and deliberate exclusion of certain categories of patient —for example, those living in temporary accommodation. The increased emphasis on the capitation component in general practitioners' remuneration may help to remove some of these constraints in some areas, but if some practices are made uneconomic as a consequence the range of alternatives on offer will be reduced. Constraints which differentially affect particular groups of consumers include the availability of transport, financial resources, time, work commitments, family commitments, etc. As a consequence some people have potential access to a much greater range of alternatives than others.

It is not clear whether the proponents of the market model wish to encourage diversity or uniformity. On the one hand, they tend to talk about the need to provide consumers with a range of choices; on the other hand, they wish to promote uniformly high standards of care. The market mechanism tends to be good at producing diversity—as, for example, in the range of restaurants available—but perhaps less good at producing uniform standards of excellence. British general practice is already characterised by extreme diversity in every aspect of provision and patterns of care. Do we expect greater consumer sovereignty to encourage this diversity or reduce it?

Information

If consumers have the motivation to exercise choice and a range of alternatives from which to choose, they then require adequate information about those alternatives. The white paper says that practices will be encouraged to produce and distribute information about the services they offer. But research shows a low level of demand for information from consumers when choosing a new doctor. Ritchie reported that 70% of patients did not want to know anything about the organisation or the size of the prospective practice. Only one in 10 wanted to know whether there was an appointments system, what surgery times were, how available doctors were, or whether the practice ran special clinics.[2]

Many practices already provide basic information about such aspects of their work as surgery hours and arrangements, but few say much about the doctors, except perhaps their names and their qualifications (usually without explanation). Many would be reluctant to provide more information, and there would be problems in deciding what information was relevant and useful. Should practices, for example, provide information about their prescribing habits or referral rates? If such information were available how much use would it be to patients faced with a choice between practice A and practice B?

For those consumers who want information the problem is one of where to obtain it. While individual practices may issue leaflets, the only central compilation of information is the family practitioner committee list of general practitioners. But a survey carried out in London reported that only one in five of those who had registered with a general practitioner in the past five years had even heard of the family practitioner committee.[7] The information provided by family practitioner committees is variable but generally limited and its distribution is haphazard. For example, only one in six family practitioner committees provide information about daytime reception cover.[8] The prospect of more sophisticated information being routinely available to patients seems fairly remote.

Competence to make a choice

The market mechanism is an effective means of improving standards only if consumers are capable of making rational decisions, having weighed the benefits and costs of the available alternatives. A fundamental problem inherent in the view of the patient as a consumer is that the service provided is only an imperfect means to the desired end. The commodity sought by patients is health, not medical care per se. While patients may be the best judges of this desired commodity they may not possess the necessary competence to judge the quality of care provided. Despite the fact that this argument has rightly aroused suspicion when it has been used by doctors as a means of sustaining professional power, it remains a strong argument. If the judgment of a doctor's technical competence to distinguish between a minor self limiting

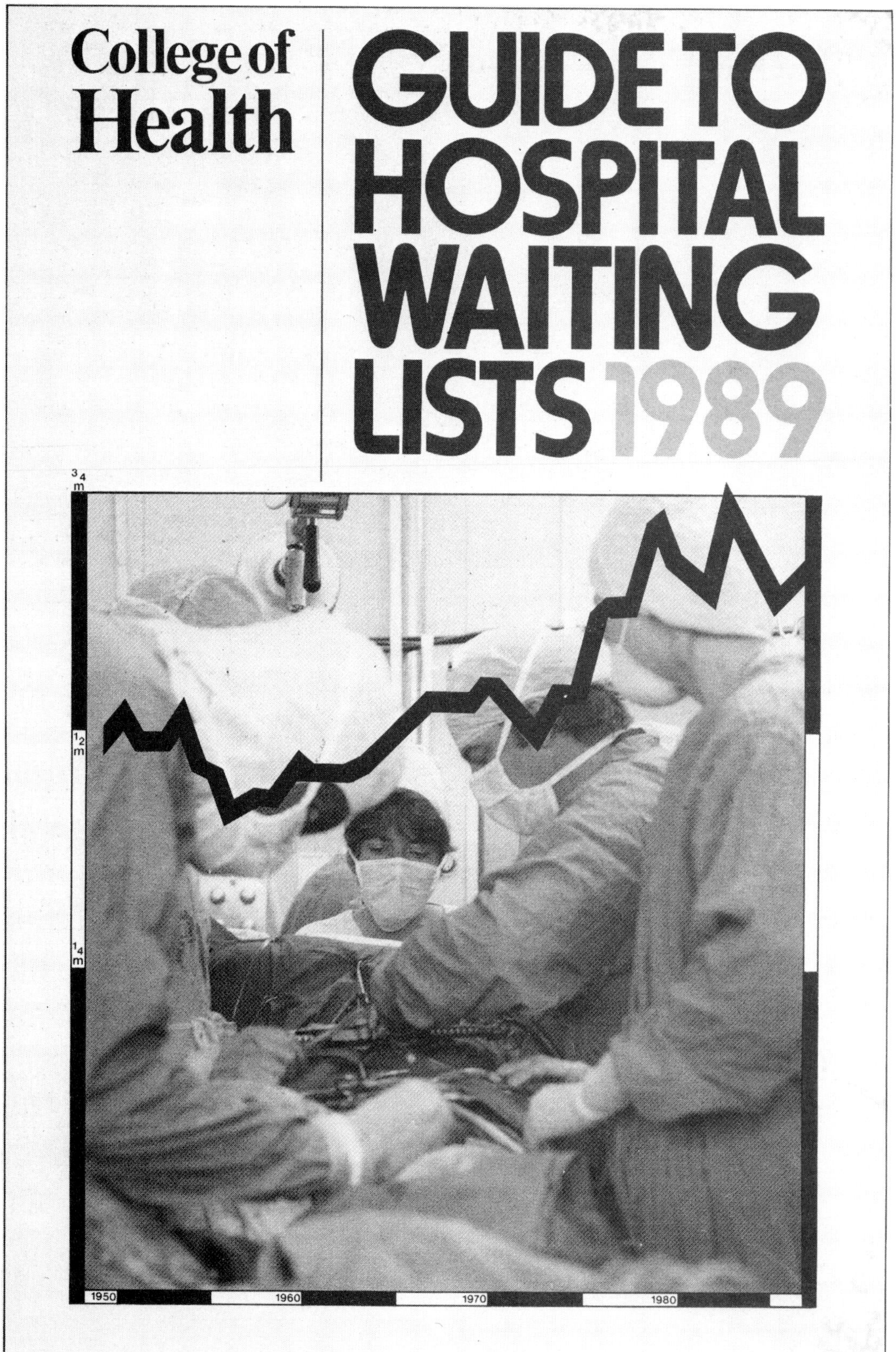

College of Health

GUIDE TO HOSPITAL WAITING LISTS 1989

18

complaint and a serious life threatening illness relies only on the patient's assessment of final outcome the consumer may find that it is too late to exercise choice.

There are, of course, many aspects of general practice about which consumers are perfectly competent to make a choice, including characteristics of the doctor, surgery hours, availability of clinics, appointment systems, surgery facilities, other services, etc. It would, however, be unfortunate if these were to be elevated above clinical competence in the desire to enhance consumer sovereignty.

If all other conditions are met and the consumer is able to make a choice there remains the need to provide an opportunity to implement that choice. The proposal to allow patients to change their doctors without approaching their existing general practitioners or the family practitioner committee is a welcome step towards enabling them to implement choices. Nevertheless, even with the removal of restrictive procedures, the registration system will remain a constraint.

> ## ". . . the market mechanism is effective only if consumers are capable of making rational decisions."

Changing doctors will still require patients to go through a formal procedure. Unlike consumers of other goods and services consumers of health care are unable to sample alternatives or to use a different supplier as and when they think it is appropriate. Without abandoning the undoubted advantages of the registered population, and thus transforming the organisation of health care under the NHS (with a consequent increase in cost), registration requirements will remain an obstacle to consumers' freedom to exercise choice.

Scope for consumerism in general practice

The proposals advanced by ministers owe more to political ideology and rhetoric than they do to an analysis of how people actually set about choosing a doctor. The little evidence we have suggests that few people behave in the way implied by the classic market model. Surveys show that convenience and tradition rather than an evaluation of available alternatives largely determine the choice of general practitioner. Most people inherit their doctor or simply choose the nearest practice. Only a minority take into account a recommendation, and this is usually from friends, relatives, or neighbours.[2-4] Once registered there is little incentive to change. Ritchie et al reported that four out of five adults had been with their present practice for five years or more and during a year only 4% had registered with a new doctor.[2] Most people

change doctors only when circumstances force them to do so rather than for positive reasons, such as the possibility of obtaining a better standard of service elsewhere.

The issue of choice might be expected to be more relevant in the American system, where market forces can play a much greater role. Kronenfeld reported that nearly 60% of the people in her United States sample named two or more doctors practising in different locations as their "regular" doctors.[9] This implies that American patients have far greater opportunity to shop around and compare the alternatives on offer. A recent study, however, found that fewer than 40% of people surveyed engaged in consumerist behaviours, which were defined as willingness to seek out information, readiness to exercise independent judgment, and readiness to make quality comparisons when selecting a doctor.[10] This suggests that any move to increase consumer choice in Britain, starting from a much lower threshold, is likely to face considerable inertia. Whatever its applicability in other areas of the provision of services, we believe that the market mechanism is unlikely to yield any dramatic improvements in the quality or efficiency of general practitioner care. This is not to suggest that we disagree with the government's objective of making general practitioner services more responsive to the needs and wishes of consumers or of raising standards of practice.

We believe that these objectives will not be realised by simple reliance on individual consumer choice, at least within the confines of the present system. There are other ways in which the collective wishes of consumers of health care can be expressed and in which the quality of care can be improved. In this context we welcome proposals to increase the role of medical audit in ensuring high quality care.

It is unfortunate but perhaps not surprising that the white paper contains no proposals to enhance the power of consumers collectively to influence the service through community health councils or increased representation on family practitioner committees. There are no solutions which will solve all problems at a stroke, and it would be naive of ministers to assume that the application of market principles will achieve major improvements in primary health care.

1 Secretaries of State for Health, Wales, Northern Ireland, and Scotland. *Working for patients.* London: HMSO, 1989. (Cmnd 555.)
2 Ritchie J, Jacoby A, Bone M. *Access to primary health care.* London: HMSO, 1981.
3 Simpson R. Access to primary care. *Royal Commission on the NHS/National Consumer Council research paper No. 6.* London: HMSO, 1979.
4 Cartwright A, Anderson R. *General practice revisited: a second study of patients and their doctors.* London: Tavistock, 1981.
5 College of Health. *Comments on primary health care discussion paper.* London: College of Health, 1987.
6 Butler JR, Knight R. Medical practice areas in England: some facts and figures. *Health Trends* 1976;8:8-12.
7 Bone M. *Registration with general medical practitioners in inner London.* London: HMSO, 1984.
8 Dennis H, Havelock G. How easily can practices be contracted during normal working hours? *J R Coll Gen Pract* 1988;38(306):32-3.
9 Kronenfeld JJ. Organisation of ambulatory care by consumers. *Sociology of Health and Illness.* 1982;4:183-200.
10 Hibbard JH, Weeks EC. Consumerism in health care—prevalence and predictors. *Medical Care* 1987;25(11):1019-32.

Indicative drug budgets for general practitioners

Bernie O'Brien

Given that the drugs bill is the single largest item of family practitioner service expenditure and that in the past there has been little incentive for GPs to consider these costs in terms of frequency or context, the white paper proposes indicative drug budgets. These will be set by family practitioner committees (FPC) for individual practices using a weighted capitation formula, which may be extended for local social and epidemiological factors. Joint formularies between FPCs and hospitals in an NHS district will be encouraged, regular monitoring of prescribing will be introduced, and in an incentive scheme the FPC may keep half the savings within the area.

Little indication is given about how the effectiveness of the proposals will be evaluated. In particular, cost containment is an inadequate measure and data on the quality of patient care and its outcomes will be needed.

The white paper *Working for Patients* was published in January[1]; the eight working papers followed nearly a month later. Working paper No 4 explains the reasoning behind the proposals to give general practitioners indicative prescribing budgets.[2] The perceived problem and the objective of the new policy are stated concisely:

It is generally recognised that some prescribing is wasteful or unnecessarily expensive. The objective of the new arrangements is to place downward pressure on expenditure on drugs in order to eliminate this waste and to release resources for other parts of the health service.

The problem

Expenditure on the family practitioner services was just over £5 billion in 1987-8 and the services account for 24% of total NHS spending. At £1·9 billion, the drugs bill is the single largest item of family practitioner services expenditure: in any given year more is spent on medicines than on the doctors who prescribe them.

"... the government is treating the symptoms of health care cost inflation rather than the cause."

Although the proportion of NHS expenditure on pharmaceuticals has remained fairly constant over the past 25 years, the aging population and the introduction of new and more expensive medicines is creating upward pressure on the drugs bill.

The problem is not simply a concern with the absolute level of spending; the question is an evaluative one of value for money or cost effectiveness. The belief underlying the present proposals is that the prescribing of medicines could be more cost effective—that is, the same level of patient benefits could be generated but at a lower level of expenditure. Similar economic reasoning can be found in the earlier primary care white paper where it was claimed that the introduction of the selected list in 1985, restricting the availability of several products on NHS prescription, resulted in an annual saving of £75m, and that this saving was achieved without detriment to patient care.[3]

But when a government seeks to restrict arbitrarily for cost reasons which products may be prescribed by general practitioners it is treating the symptoms of health care cost inflation rather than the cause. At the heart of the problem is the fact that general practitioners have had little incentive in the past to consider the costs of their prescribing either in terms of its frequency or content. Unlike the cash limited hospital sector, where there is a strong incentive for pharmacies to dispense cheaper generic equivalents rather than brand name drugs, the financial consequences of higher prescribing costs are not borne by individual family practitioner committees or general practitioner practices. Such general practitioner prescribing freedom has contributed to wide differences in prescribing practices and costs which cannot be wholly explained in terms of patient demography and morbidity. In 1986-7, for example, drug expenditures varied from £26 per head of population in one family practitioner committee to £40 in another,[1] and variability between general practitioner practices is likely to be even greater.

The proposed solution to the problem is that by giving general practitioners prescribing budgets, in addition to the detailed information on their prescribing habits already planned under the primary care white paper, the incentives for cost conscious prescribing are created.

The proposals

● Regional health authorities will be allocated annual budgets to cover expenditure on medicines and appliances in the family practitioner services within the region. Remuneration for pharmacies and dispensing doctors will not be included in drug budgets nor will budgets take account of income from prescription charges. Regional health authorities will pass on drug budgets to family practitioner committees, which will be responsible for setting indicative drug budgets for individual practices. (Those with lists of more than 11 000 who have elected to receive practice budgets will have an allowance within this for drugs.)

● After a period of transition allocations to regional health authorities and family practitioner committees will be on the basis of resident population using a weighted capitation formula. Factors in the allocation formula will include the age and sex of patients, morbidity, temporary residents, and cross boundary flows. The relative weights to be attached to these

Health Economics Research Group, Brunel University, Middlesex UB8 3PH
Bernie O'Brien, MSC, research fellow

Br Med J 1989;298:944-6

factors and the addition of other factors deemed relevant are yet to be determined.

● The weighted capitation formula will also form the basis for family practitioner committees setting indicative budgets for general practitioner practices. Again the formula may be extended to allow for local social and epidemiological factors that may influence the demand for drugs. Furthermore, the working paper notes that factors such as referral rates of patients to hospital, special interests of practices, and patients in need of unusually expensive medicines will need to be taken into account.

● The level at which the family practitioner committee sets an indicative drug budget for an individual practice will depend on the factors outlined above and a comparison of the practice's current prescribing with the average level for broadly comparable practices in the same family practitioner committee. "Generally, where the current level is higher than the average, the indicative budget will be set somewhere between the two figures" (para 2.5). Therefore the overall aim of the procedures is to bring downward pressure on practices with above average prescribing costs where the differences in prescribing "cannot be explained by the composition of their practice lists or other accepted factors."

● Joint formularies between family practitioner committees and hospitals in an NHS district are to be encouraged so that "both hospital doctors and general practitioners are guided to use the same medicines."

● General practitioner practices will be required to monitor their prescribing and cost information and provide monthly returns to the family practitioner committee; in turn the family practitioner committees must develop information systems for monitoring and comparing the activity and cost data across general practitioner practices.

● An incentive scheme will operate. General practitioner practices in a family practitioner committee can aim for expenditure lower than the drug budget allocated to the family practitioner committee by the region, and where such targets are achieved the family practitioner committee will keep half the savings to be spent on primary care improvement schemes within the committee's area.

Is your repeat prescription really cost effective? Fewer prescriptions may mean longer consultations

● Where general practitioner practices overspend on indicative drug budgets a process of discussion with the family practitioner committee and peer review will

be entered into, and if this fails the ultimate sanction is to withhold remuneration from the doctors concerned.

Bold prescription for change

The proposals offer a bold prescription for change. Taken in conjunction with the proposed policy of realigning family practitioner committees to be accountable to regional health authorities, drug budgeting and the other general practitioner reforms offer an important step towards the integration of primary care with the rest of the NHS in terms of resource allocation, management, and accountability.

The indicative drug budget proposals are designed to build on the Prescribing Analysis and Cost information system proposed in the earlier primary care white paper. The working paper claims that this quarterly feedback to general practitioners on their prescribing and costs from the Prescription Pricing Authority "has increased awareness among general practitioners of the cost of their prescribing decisions." Indeed, there is some evidence which suggests that, even without the use of budgets, such passive information feedback can modify prescribing behaviour in some doctors.[4] A good example of differential cost awareness can be found with dispensing general practitioners compared with their non-dispensing colleagues: data for 1986 indicate that, although these groups have the same prescribing rate per caput (7.1), the net ingredient cost per prescription is lower for doctors who dispense their own medicines and are aware of such costs.[5][6] But, although awareness may generate self audit and modified prescribing among the motivated minority, the burden of evidence from hospital studies of feeding back cost information to doctors is that raised awareness is a necessary but not sufficient condition for behaviour change.[7] Correspondingly, the current proposals endorse the view that such feedback needs to be reinforced with budgetary incentives and sanctions.

Although the idea of drug budgets for general practitioners has been around for some time,[8] the present proposals state that budgets will be indicative rather than binding. This careful qualification sounds an understandable note of caution in expectation of the difficulties of setting drug budgets using weighted capitation formulae. Population characteristics may explain only part of the variation in prescribing; several studies have shown that a range of characteristics of doctors are correlated with prescribing behaviour in addition to external influences such as promotion by the pharmaceutical industry.[9][10] Given such statistical uncertainties, a good deal of flexibility will be built into the process of budget setting. As is currently the case in the policing of prescribing by regional medical officers, a key focus will be how far above average a practice's

> **"... lower list sizes will simply result in more, rather than longer, consultations."**

prescribing is when compared with similar practices in the area, and whether the excess can be explained in terms of the composition of practice lists or other factors.

The weighted capitation formula is a key element in the proposed allocation criteria and is similar in conception to the Resource Allocation Working Party's formula for revenue allocations to NHS regions (although this too will be simplified under the white paper proposals).[11] The rationale is that variation in the need for prescription drugs can be adequately modelled as a function of population characteristics for the purpose of budget allocations. But factors such as age and sex are more easily measured than others such as morbidity, although this latter may explain a significant proportion of prescribing variance. No guidance is given as to what measures of morbidity would be used. Standardised mortality rates are unlikely to be good predictors of primary care prescribing, but alternatives such as general practitioner consultation rates are measures of utilisation and workload rather than morbidity. An important feature of the morbidity measure(s) chosen to reflect prescribing costs is that it is sensitive to the prevalence as well as to the incidence of disease. In 1986, for example, the net ingredient cost of drugs for chronic conditions such as rheumatism is £8.88 per item compared with £3.18 for drugs to treat infections.

Need for longer consultations?

The predicted impact of drug budgets is that they will create an incentive for the general practitioner to reduce the frequency of prescribing and to substitute less costly (typically generic) items for the more expensive brand name products. Generic substitution of equivalent efficacy drugs creates no obvious additional burden for the general practitioner, except in remembering some of the more complex generic names. (The long term impact of generic substitution on drug industry research and development is a subject for another debate.) But attempting to reduce the rate of prescribing, without an adverse impact on the quality of care, may require the substitution of some other factor in its place, such as the general practitioners' time in a longer period of consultation.[12] Although the decline in average list sizes—from 2291 patients per doctor in 1976 to 1988 in 1986—might enable consultations to extend beyond the average six minutes,[13] recent survey evidence suggests that lower list sizes will simply result in more, rather than longer, consultations.[14] Furthermore, there is an obvious concern that unless the budget criteria fully compensate for high drug cost patients (in type or number of scripts), such patients may not be viewed by general practitioners as attractive additions to their list.

The family practitioner committee is the focal point for the exercise of financial incentives and sanctions. It is the family practitioner committee which keeps half the difference of any underspend against the drug budget set by the region. What is not clear from the working paper is whether the reward is for aggregated underspending by a family practitioner committee or whether all general practitioner practices should have an expenditure outturn within, say, 5% of budget. The sanction of last resort against those practices which overspend on their drug budget is to withhold doctors' remuneration. Such action is likely to create some interesting contractual problems because it is the individual doctor who is in contract with the family practitioner committee but the practice which will hold the indicative drug budget.

In conclusion, little indication is given in the working paper as to how the success or failure of the proposals will be evaluated. If the test is to be one of improved cost effectiveness the monitoring of reduced drug expenditure alone is inadequate. Data are required on the quality of patient care and treatment outcomes to determine whether they can be maintained, or even improved, at lower cost. The proposals are to be tried out in 1990-1; I hope that comparative trials will be designed to address questions of effectiveness as well as of cost.

1 Secretaries of State for Health, Wales, Northern Ireland, and Scotland. *Working for patients*. London: HMSO, 1989. (Cmnd 555.)
2 Secretaries of State for Health, Wales, Northern Ireland, and Scotland. *Indicative prescribing budgets for general medical practitioners. Working paper 4*. London: HMSO, 1989.
3 Secretaries of State for Social Services, Wales, Northern Ireland, and Scotland. *Promoting better health*. London: HMSO, 1987. (Cmnd 249.)
4 Harris CM, Jarman B, Woodman E, White P, Fry JS. *Prescribing—a suitable case for treatment*. London: Royal College of General Practitioners, 1984.
5 Department of Health and Social Security. *Statistics for general medical practitioners in England and Wales: 1976 to 1986*. London: Government Statistical Service, 1988.
6 Office of Health Economics. *Compendium of health statistics*. 6th ed. London: Office of Health Economics, 1987.
7 Wickings I, Coles JM, Flux R, Howard L. Review of clinical budgeting and costing experiments. *Br Med J* 1983;286:575-7.
8 Wade OL. Prescribing. In: Phillips CI, Wolfe JN, eds. *Clinical practice and economics*. London: Pitman Medical, 1976.
9 Hemminki E. Review of the literature on the factors affecting drug prescribing. *Social Science and Medicine* 1975;9:111-5.
10 Worthen DB. Prescribing influences: an overview. *British Journal of Medical Education* 1973;7:109-17.
11 Department of Health and Social Security. *Sharing resources for health in England. Report of the Resource Allocation Working Party*. London: HMSO, 1976.
12 Murray TS, Barber JH, Hannay DR. Consulting time and prescribing rates. *Update* 1978;16:969-75.
13 Wilson AD. Consultation length: general practitioners' attitudes and practices. *Br Med J* 1985;290:1322-4.
14 Butler JR, Calnan MW. List sizes and use of time in general practice. *Br Med J* 1987;295:1383-6.

The new general practitioner contract

David Morrell

General practice could be improved by non-radical changes that do not threaten clinical freedom. Practices should contract with the family practitioner committee (FPC) to provide services for a defined community to defined standards. The basic practice allowance should be increased, but in line with the services provided and on condition that an annual practice report is published. Thus practices could be graded on a scale from 1 to 5, with those graded 1 receiving no allowance and those graded 5 twice the average. A paid audit committee appointed by the FPC should visit each practice every two years, evaluating premises, equipment, records, team work, services, teaching and research, services to the NHS, prescribing, and particular problems in inner city and rural work. Such a system would achieve the objectives of the white paper, which currently ignores perhaps the most crucial aspect of primary care: the time doctors can spend in listening to and counselling their patients.

The National Health Service at its best is without equal. Time and again the nation has seen just how much we owe to those who work in it.

But major tasks now face us, to bring all parts of the National Health Service up to the very high standard of the best, while maintaining the principles on which it is founded and to prepare for the needs of the future.

There is evidence of widespread agreement with these statements from the Prime Minister, among both the receivers and providers of health care. The increasing negative reaction that has been generated by the white paper *Working for Patients*[1] and the new general practitioner contract[2] does not appear to have been based on a reluctance to consider change but rather on a deep concern that the proposals will not only fail to achieve their stated objectives for patient care but, on the contrary, will be harmful to the functioning of the health services. There is no place for complacency about the delivery of health care in the United Kingdom, and the publication of these documents provides a valuable and perhaps necessary stimulus for urgent rethinking. The challenge that faces all of those concerned with the delivery of health care is to ensure that the result of this process is an improvement in the services provided.

The Secretary of State has indicated that, although he will not accept procrastination, he will accept positive proposals, and it is with this in mind that I make the following proposals from the perspective of general practice.

The role of general practice

The general practitioner is concerned with providing care for populations of individuals who have registered with him or her for primary care. This care includes:

- Responding to new requests for care from patients by identifying their problems and taking appropriate management decisions, which may include giving advice, prescribing treatment, or referral to secondary care
- The continuing care of chronic disease and aging processes and the care of terminally ill and bereaved patients
- Appropriate screening and health education
- Prevention—primary, secondary, and tertiary.

Good quality general practitioner care demands:

- Provision of adequate premises for the delivery of care and appropriate equipment
- Maintenance of good records of the care provided
- Age and sex registers of the population for which the doctor is responsible with the facility to identify particularly vulnerable groups in the population
- Provision of services for patients with special needs, such as antenatal care, contraceptive care, well baby clinics, and immunisation, and care of the elderly and supervision of those with certain chronic disorders, such as diabetes, hypertension, etc
- Development of a team approach to providing comprehensive primary care services.

Good quality general practitioner care does not demand:

- Responsibility for the control of people's behaviour, be this concerned with excessive eating, smoking, sexual promiscuity, or drug taking. These are the responsibilities of society at large, and to impose such a responsibility on the general practitioner is to condone the medicalisation of social behaviour, warned against by Ivan Illich[3]
- Provision of routine medical examinations for healthy adults. These have not been shown to improve health, and there is some evidence that they increase anxiety, morbid preoccupation with disease, and absence from work.

The new contract for general practitioners must be viewed with these basic principles in mind. Certain standards of performance have been determined that are concerned almost entirely with preventive care, some of which is of questionable benefit. Some of these standards seem to ignore the rights of patients to accept or reject care. Other aspects of the contract with respect to preventive services totally ignore the problems of calculating appropriate denominators in order to measure the percentage response to care. Overall, the contract is imbued with the belief that "good care," as it defines it, will attract more patients to the doctors providing this care, and the doctors will consequently receive greater financial rewards through a system of payment based largely on capitation. It ignores perhaps the most crucial aspect of primary care, which is concerned with the time doctors can devote to listening to and identifying their patients' problems and to providing counselling, advice, health education, and appropriate management.

The doctor trained to provide care under the new contract will employ an array of nurses and

Division of General Practice, United Medical and Dental Schools of Guy's and St Thomas's Hospitals, London SE11 6SP
David Morrell, FRCGP, *professor of general practice*

Br Med J 1989;298:1005-7

health educators. Patients entering the consulting room will be screened, advised about their weight, smoking habits, stress level, immunisation state, etc. Unfortunately some of these patients may have illnesses that can be diagnosed and treated appropriately only if the doctor takes time to listen to their problems, examine and investigate them, and respond to their current needs. The competition for capitation fees may make it difficult for the doctor to respond in this manner.

Is there an alternative?

On the whole, doctors in general practice sympathise with the government's objective of bringing all parts of the NHS "up to the very high standard of the best." This is a standard that the Prime Minister herself acknowledges is without equal in the world, and it has been achieved with the current contractual arrangements. It is how NHS staff members can be encouraged to achieve this standard that is the issue that must be debated. Will the radical changes proposed in the new contract really have the effect of bringing inferior standards of practice up to the level of the best? This is questionable. The emphasis on income derived from capitation fees will encourage the development of large lists of patients. The emphasis on prevention means that doctors who wish to earn maximum fees for their services will be constrained to show adherence to totally unrealistic indicators of performance. Doctors who provide a caring and compassionate service, which takes time but is much less easily audited, will have an appreciable disincentive to provide the care that patients value.

Improvements in general practice could be achieved by simple changes that do not entail a radical overhaul of the present contract. These changes, however, do demand a change of heart in the profession but not one that will in any way threaten clinical freedom. They can be achieved by accepting the concept that general practitioners should contract with the family practitioner committee to provide services for a defined community of patients to a standard defined by the committee in consultation with the profession and consumer associations. In return for this agreement the general practitioner would be paid a basic practice allowance for the services provided and a capitation fee for each registered patient, with a higher fee for elderly patients. Rather than reducing the basic practice allowance it should be increased, but it should be dictated by the services provided. As part of the contract each practice would be constrained to provide

Above average practices should keep routine blood pressure records for at least 50% of patients aged over 40

the family practitioner committee with an annual report of the services provided, which could be audited by comparison with items of service payments, and each practice would be visited at intervals of two years by an audit committee. The facts provided in the annual report, together with the report of the audit committee, should lead to a grading for each practice from poor to excellent, on the basis of which the basic practice allowance for the next two years could be calculated.

Auditing services

In order to obtain the mean basic practice allowance general practitioners should be expected to provide those services that have been shown to be or by common consent may be accepted as necessary for providing good quality medical care. Extra services that may enhance the basic practice allowance should also be restricted to services that have been shown to enhance patient care, either directly or through the efficient use of resources. Services that are conducive to the development of general practice, the health service, research, or education should be given due recognition. Services such as routine medical examinations for healthy adults that have not been shown to enhance the quality of health and, indeed, in some studies have led to a deterioration in health should not be included in evaluations. New services should not be provided unless they are established on a sound research footing.

Services to be evaluated by the audit committee

A prerequisite for paying any basic practice allowance would be the provision of an annual practice report. From this basic and extra services would be identified and graded, and these may subsequently be verified by visitors from the audit committee. I suggest that the following services should be considered when the grading for the basic practice allowance is judged. My suggestions are based on a combination of common sense and research evidence concerning the provision of good quality general practitioner care. Because the main concern in this audit is with raising the quality of the most inferior services the standards proposed are not particularly demanding.

Premises—Good and sympathetic care cannot be provided in the absence of adequate consulting and waiting rooms. These should include: adequate waiting space determined according to the number of registered patients; adequate heating and lighting; toilet facilities for patients; a consulting room of defined minimal size; an examination couch and washing facilities; facilities for sterilising instruments and disposing waste; and storage of emergency drugs and equipment.

Equipment—Basic diagnostic equipment, including an auroscope, an ophthalmoscope, a vaginal speculum, a proctoscope, a peak flow meter, and a weighing machine should be available. Equipment for simple surgical procedures, such as scalpels, scissors, and forceps, and for simple diagnostic procedures, such as diagnostic strip tests for urine, syringes, needles, laboratory containers, and cervical cytology equipment, should be basic to any practice. The possession of extra equipment, such as an electrocardiograph, an electric cautery, a cryocautery, and a nebuliser, should be expected in practices with an above average grading.

Records—Each practice should have an age-sex register that is updated properly. Each consultation should be entered in the medical records, with details of the patient's problem, its management, and drugs prescribed. All practices should provide drug records for patients receiving repeat prescriptions. There should be evidence in the records that patients who are receiving treatment with steroids, antihypertensive drugs, diuretics, or hypoglycaemic drugs are seen at least once every six months. All above average practices would be expected to keep routine blood pressure records for at least 50% of the patients over the age of 40 and have computers with call and recall systems for immunisations and cervical smear tests.

Team work—A team approach, either by attached nursing and health visiting staff or by well developed liaison with nurses and health visitors, should be evident. This could be confirmed in auditing by consulting the community nursing services. The provision of a practice nurse, a dietitian, and a psychologist might be looked for in practices graded above average.

Services—In addition to services provided on demand and continuing care for chronic disease, practices should provide well baby and immunisation services, out of hours care, antenatal care (either on a community or a shared care basis), and family planning services. The provision of these services can be confirmed by item of service payments. Special screening for the elderly, community obstetric or diabetic care, community psychiatric services, etc, might be expected in practices given an above average grading.

Teaching and research—Practices selected by peer review to provide undergraduate teaching and vocational training and to carry out research might expect a higher than average grading.

Services to the health service—General practitioners committed to work designed to advance general practitioner care nationally, such as members of district committees, Royal College of General Practitioners committees, BMA committees, etc, might expect a higher than average grading.

Patterns of prescribing—Prescribing profiles for practices will be available to the family practitioner committee, and practices in which the profile indicates prescribing costs of 20% or more above the district average should be investigated. The results of the investigation could influence the grading for the basic practice allowance of such a practice.

Inner city and rural practices—Some practices, particularly in inner cities, experience a very high turnover of patients, which leads to an increased workload. Wide dispersal of patients in rural areas also presents special problems. These factors should be taken into account when practices are graded.

Evaluation of services provided

On the basis of annual reports, item of service payments, visits by the audit committee, and prescribing profiles, practices could be graded from poor to excellent on a scale of 1 to 5. Those graded 1 would receive no basic practice allowance; those graded 5 would receive twice the average allowance. In this way the services provided could be related to remuneration.

As a result of supervision the services might be expected to improve and costs would go up. This is entirely in keeping with the government's aims for a better service. In time, however, all practices might be expected to have computers and practice nurses, and it may be necessary to modify the basic service expected in general practice to attract the mean basic practice allowance. In due course new initiatives in prevention and services may be proved to be desirable, and these could then be incorporated into the services expected in order to attract a mean basic practice allowance. With advances in information systems all practices will probably need a computer, and an initiative by the government to provide this facility will become necessary.

The audit committee

The appointment of the audit committee will be crucial to the success of this programme, and it is important that people appointed to this committee are trusted by the doctors working in the community. At the same time it is important that the government should see the members of the audit committee as independent assessors of the services being provided. I propose that the audit committee should be appointed by the family practitioner committee and should include a general practitioner nominated by the local medical committee, a community nurse, a manager from the family practitioner committee, a community doctor (with special responsibility for organising and interpreting data), and a lay chairman. All members appointed to this committee should be agreed by the local medical committee; they should be paid for their services and be expected to devote one day each week to committee work. This should make it possible for them to visit each practice every two years. A mechanism for appeal should be available to doctors who disagree with their grading, but this should be based only on questions of fact, which should, however, include questions concerned with the age and sex structure of a practice. Practices with totally inadequate premises would have to be supported by loans to improve the premises if they are to be protected from a vicious circle of lack of finance and further deterioration in grading.

This system of audit will meet most of the government's wishes to improve the quality of general practitioner care, bringing all parts of the NHS "up to the very high standard of the best." It would not challenge the doctor-patient relationship by introducing financial factors to decision making. Above all it would not allow financial considerations to interfere with the day to day conduct of general practitioner care; nor would it encourage general practitioners to provide care for very large lists of patients in order to satisfy their greed.

Conclusion

I have described ways in which general practitioners may be constrained to provide care that is sensitive to the quality of the services provided. Individual items of service would continue to attract remuneration and thus encourage good practice. Basic clinical care would be encouraged through audit of records and prescribing. Seniority payments could be linked to postgraduate training. The overemphasis on prevention in the new contract, which is just a part of the general practitioner's normal services, could largely be delegated to nurses and would be balanced by good general care and not constrained by unrealistic targets related to unreliable denominators.

Such a system would achieve the objectives of *Working for Patients*. If the profession supported this it would be seen to be behind the objectives of the new contract. If the profession is not prepared to accept some form of external audit after years of failing to provide a satisfactory internal audit then it probably deserves the treatment the government is proposing. If the government rejects the system it would clearly indicate that its prime concern is with an ideology concerned with the market place, a misunderstanding of the principles on which general practice is founded, and a total disregard for patient care. The electorate has then a clear decision to make. To someone who has dedicated a professional lifetime to studying and developing the role of the general practitioner and improving his or her status this would be profoundly disappointing.

1 Secretaries of State for Health, Wales, Northern Ireland, and Scotland. *Working for patients.* London: HMSO, 1989. (Cmnd 555.)
2 Department of Health and Welsh Office. *General practice in the National Health Service. A new contract.* London: DHSS, 1989.
3 Illich I. *Medical nemesis: the expropriation of health.* London: Calder and Boyars, 1975.

Quality and the use of time in general practice

J G R Howie, A M D Porter, J F Forbes

To examine the association between different consulting styles in general practice (defined according to the average length of doctor-patient contact time in surgery consultations) and the process of care for those patients presenting with new episodes of respiratory illness, 1787 consultations conducted by 85 general practitioner principals in Lothian from November 1987 to May 1988 were analysed. Short as against long consultations resulted in less attention being given to psychosocial issues that the doctor recognised as relevant. When psychosocial problems were dealt with prescribing of antibiotics decreased. In this volunteer sample of doctors the process of care seemed to reflect decisions as to how time was allocated rather than inherently different patterns of clinical behaviour.

Organisational and contractural changes will shift the mix of financial and professional incentives for general practitioners in ways that could lead to doctors reallocating their time towards shorter consultations; such a reallocation could have important implications for patient care.

The National Health Service is facing its most significant overhaul in its 40 year history. Two white papers and eight working documents raise points of principle, structure, and detail that are in need of thoughtful but urgent debate; but this is complicated by a shortage of clearly apposite data.[1][2]

The debate is made more difficult by the problem of defining quality or goodness of doctoring. Much of the important research in primary care in recent years has focused on the issues of list size and the use of time. The green paper that preceded the white paper on primary care pointed to the absence of consistent and substantial evidence that list size was related to quality of care,[3] although recently it has been shown that doctors with smaller lists generally have longer consultations.[4] Other work has shown that longer consultations include more health education[5] and are associated with different prescribing decisions.[6]

We have recently completed the main data collection in a 12 month study exploring variables that may link or intervene between the quality and quantity of care. We looked at "consulting style" (defined as average time doctors spent in face to face consultation), length of consultation, and quality of care. We used as proxies for quality the extent to which psychosocial problems that had been identified as relevant at consultations for respiratory problems were explored and how antibiotics were prescribed. The first six months of data were used for this paper; decisions taken relating to those patients who consulted with new episodes of respiratory illness were used for comparisons.

Subjects and methods

Eighty five (of 496) general practitioner principals in Lothian recorded information on their work on one day in 15 for a year. (A Monday recording day was followed progressively by a Tuesday, a Wednesday, and so on). Information was collected about features of practice organisation both generally and in relation to individual recording days. The flow of patients into and out of the consulting room was noted, as was the time of patients' arrival at the doctors' surgeries and, when relevant, their actual appointment times. Doctors recorded details of the patients' problems and their management on separate cards.

All diagnoses recorded were classified by experienced coders using the Royal College of General Practitioners' classification.[7] For this study "respiratory illnesses" included all patients in the respiratory illness section of the classification together with those diagnosed as having a cough, sore throat, otitis media, streptococcal sore throat, and viral illness not otherwise specified. Patients diagnosed as having asthma or chronic bronchitis were excluded.

The psychosocial component of each consultation was categorised by the doctors into one of four options: none relevant, present but not dealt with, dealt with a little, or dealt with in depth. This classification was arrived at after a pilot study that sought to strike a balance between detail and conciseness. The names of drugs prescribed were recorded by the doctor and coded using a classification based on the *British National Formulary*.[8]

Doctors taking part were volunteers and constituted 17% of all general practitioners in the Lothian area and represented 43% of practices in the area. Twenty one of the 85 doctors were women, and all kinds of practice (from singlehanded to six doctor partnerships) were represented. In most large practices the doctors restricted the number of partners taking part to reduce the load on their clerical staff.

The average time each doctor spent on individual consultations was calculated for the first six months of the study (November 1987 to May 1988). Nineteen doctors consulting for an average of nine minutes or more per patient were categorised as "slower" doctors, 25 doctors consulting for six minutes or less as "faster," and the remaining 41 as "intermediate."

The 19 slower doctors recorded information on 2131 surgery consultations on 141 recording days. The 25 faster doctors recorded information on 4380 surgery consultations on 200 days, and the 41 intermediate doctors recorded information on 5313 surgery consultations on 301 days. Two doctors forgot to record on one of their study days, and five other days were not recorded because of new reception staff. Weekends off duty, weekdays off in lieu, and holidays accounted for most days when the doctors did not record; sickness and study leave accounted for the few remaining days.

The stated personal list sizes of the faster doctors averaged 1837 (SD 737, median 1925) whereas that for the slower doctors averaged 1512 (SD 717, median 1700). When we assessed an average figure for the practices they worked in, making allowances for all part time assistance available, the average list size of

Department of General Practice, University of Edinburgh, Edinburgh EH8 9DX
J G R Howie, MD, *professor of general practice*
A M D Porter, MPHIL, *lecturer*
J F Forbes, MSC, *research fellow*

Correspondence to:
Professor Howie.

Br Med J 1989;298:1008-10

each principal in the practices of the faster doctors was 1829 and the slower doctors 1873. Four of the faster doctors were in partnership with four of the slower doctors.

The difficulty of arriving at an average list size was compounded in that only three of the doctors in group practices claimed to operate a personal list system. None the less, table I shows an association between stated personal list size and the average length of consultation with patients. This shows a gradient running from 2169 for the doctors seeing patients for five minutes or less each to 1476 for the doctors seeing patients for nine minutes or more each.

TABLE I—*Average length of consultation and size of personal list of doctors in Lothian*

Average length of consultation	No of doctors	Average size of personal list
≤5 minutes	8	2169
-6 minutes	17	1679
-7 minutes	17	1698
-8 minutes	20	1756
-9 minutes	9	1517
>9 minutes	9	1476
Missing data	5	

The information in this paper centres on individual timings of consultations with patients, which were likely to be accurate and were constrained for error by checks against overall starting and finishing times and statements of clinical events, clinical processes, and management decisions, which required either single ticks of appropriate statements or short entries of, for example, a diagnosis or prescription.

Results

Of 11 824 consultations, 1787 (15%) were for new episodes of respiratory illnesses in the categories defined; 711 of these were undertaken by the faster doctors (16% of their consultations), 790 by the intermediate group (14% of consultations), and 286 by the slower doctors (13% of consultations). (Inconsistent denominators are due to missing information.) The results presented focus on patients seen by the faster and slower doctors.

LENGTH OF CONSULTATIONS

Of the 711 patients who saw the faster doctors, 469 (65%) had consultations that lasted six minutes or less compared with 88 (30%) of the 286 patients seen by the slower doctors. In contrast, 48 (6%) patients of the faster doctors had consultations which lasted nine minutes or more compared with 84 (29%) patients seeing slower doctors. Indeed, 13% of the consultations with the faster doctors lasted three minutes or less compared with less than 1% for the slower doctors.

PSYCHOSOCIAL COMPONENT

Table II shows the distribution of statements about the handling of psychosocial problems by all three groups of doctors. Faster doctors and slower doctors saw similar proportions of patients whom they regarded as having no relevant psychosocial problem (72% and 67% respectively). Where a relevant psychosocial problem was recognised faster doctors were less likely than slower doctors to deal with it in depth (11% v 20%; p=0·09).

PRESCRIBING OF ANTIBIOTICS

Of 701 patients seen by the faster doctors, 397 (56%) received an antibiotic compared with 141 (50%) of 277 seen by the slower doctors. In consultations lasting six minutes or less 298 of 513 (58%) patients seen by faster doctors and 49 of 95 (52%) seen by slower doctors received antibiotics. In consultations lasting nine minutes or more 27 of 56 (48%) patients of the faster and 49 of 102 (48%) patients of the slower doctors received antibiotics. Of 769 patients in the intermediate group, 383 (50%) received antibiotics; overall 921 of 1747 (52%) patients received antibiotics.

INTERRELATION OF CONSULTATION STYLE, LENGTH OF CONSULTATION, PSYCHOSOCIAL CARE, AND PRESCRIBING OF ANTIBIOTICS

Table III shows that there was a significant threefold difference in the chance of a recognised psychosocial problem being dealt with at a long consultation compared with a short consultation. There were no differences between faster and slower doctors for either long or short consultations.

Overall, the percentage of illnesses treated with antibiotics was significantly higher in patients with either no relevant psychosocial problem or a problem that was recognised but not dealt with (772 of 1418; 54%) than in patients in which the problem was recognised and dealt with (149 of 329; 45%; p<0·05) (table IV). This trend was particularly noticeable for the slower doctors.

Discussion

CLINICAL AND ORGANISATIONAL IMPLICATIONS

This study looked separately at doctors' consultation style, length of consultation, management of what the doctor saw as psychosocial problems, and prescribing of antibiotics.

Patients attending a faster compared with a slower doctor were twice as likely to have a short consultation; patients attending a slower doctor were five times as likely to have a long consultation. At long consultations a higher proportion of the psychosocial problems that were recognised were dealt with. Patients were more

TABLE II—*Identification and managements of psychosocial problems in patients presenting with respiratory illnesses to general practitioners with different consulting styles*

Consulting style of general practitioner*	No (%) of patients with no relevant psychosocial problems	Psychosocial problems dealt with in consultation (No (%) of patients):		
		Not at all	A little	In depth
Faster	506/701 (72)	76/195 (39)	98/195 (50)	21/195 (11)
Intermediate	532/770 (69)	89/238 (37)	126/238 (53)	23/238 (10)
Slower	188/281 (67)	32/93 (34)	42/93 (45)	19/93 (20)
Total	1226/1752 (70)	197/526 (37)	226/526 (51)	63/526 (12)

*Faster=average length of consultation ≤6 minutes; intermediate=7-8 minutes; slower=≥9 minutes.

TABLE III—*Management of psychosocial problems in consultations of different lengths by general practitioners with different consulting styles*

Consulting style of general practitioner*	No of patients having short consultation (≤6 mins)		No of patients having intermediate consultation (7-8 mins)		No of patients having long consultation (≥9 mins)		Total No of patients seen
	Problem not dealt with	Problem dealt with	Problem not dealt with	Problem dealt with	Problem not dealt with	Problem dealt with	
Faster	50	60	20	40	6	19	195
Slower	10	15	13	19	9	27	93
Total	60	75†	33	59†	15	46†	288

*Faster=average length of consultation ≤6 minutes; slower=≥9 minutes.
†χ^2_{trend}=6·7, df=1, p<0·01.

27

TABLE IV—*Presence and management of psychosocial problems and general practitioners' consulting style among patients prescribed antibiotics for respiratory illness. Denominators are numbers of patients with respiratory illness*

Consulting style of general practitioner*	No (%) of patients with psychosocial problem not dealt with in consultation			No (%) of patients with psychosocial problem dealt with in consultation
	No relevant problem	Problem present	Total	
Faster	299/506 (59)	45/76 (59)	344/582 (59)	53/119 (45)
Intermediate	269/531 (51)	41/89 (46)	310/620 (50)	73/149 (49)
Slower	100/187 (53)	18/29 (62)	118/216 (55)	23/61 (38)
All doctors	668/1224 (55)†	104/194 (54)†	772/1418 (54)	149/329 (45)†

*Faster=average length of consultation ≤6 minutes; intermediate=7-8 minutes; slower=≥9 minutes.
†χ^2=9·0, df=2, p=0·011.

likely to receive antibiotics when either no psychosocial problem was thought relevant or a problem that was recognised was not dealt with than when a psychosocial problem was recognised as relevant and dealt with. This was particularly so for slower doctors.

When the way in which perceived psychosocial problems are handled and how antibiotics are prescribed for patients presenting with respiratory illness are used as proxy measures of quality, short consultations seem to be less good than long consultations and faster doctoring to be associated with short consultations just as slower doctoring was associated with long consultations. Overall, faster and slower doctors recognised psychosocial problems with similar frequency. When working in short consultations they dealt similarly with these problems and prescribed similarly, and this also held true when they worked in long consultations. It thus seems reasonable to argue that quality (as defined in this paper) is a function of how competing demands on time are met rather than a function of inherently different clinical insights and behaviours.

Research into patients' views of general practice has shown that, although most patients were generally satisfied with the care they received from their doctors, they complained mainly of not having enough time with the doctor and of the doctor not listening or not explaining things properly.[9] Our conclusions seem to substantiate the subjective experience of patients.

At this early stage in the analysis of a large and complex data set it is too soon to comment in depth about what determines a fast consulting pattern. A fuller understanding of the consequences of different uses of time over a doctor's full range of activities in a working day is, however, needed before different options for the organisation or reorganisation of general practice services can be compared with regard to patients' benefit.

AUDIT AND PERFORMANCE INDICATORS

This study confirms the value of looking at information about what doctors do and predicts that it will be difficult to draw valid conclusions about quality from analysis of administrative data such as prescribing and referral statistics that are routinely collected at present. In this study an analysis of prescribing on its own would have provided little understanding of the implications of alternative strategies for providing care. Even when a fairly substantial commitment to data collecting was undertaken by a volunteer group problems of small numbers quickly handicapped analysis—for example, it would have been logical to analyse tables III and IV further in terms of each other.

More thought will be required before audit can be widely used to evaluate care in a discipline like general practice where the concepts of measurability and importance are often uneasy bedfellows.

We thank the doctors and receptionists for providing data on their daily workload, our colleagues in the Department of General Practice Research Group for their help and collaboration, and Dr Robin Prescott for statistical advice. This work was supported by grants from the Scottish Home and Health Department and the Nuffield Provincial Hospitals Trust.

1 Secretaries of State for Health, Wales, Northern Ireland, and Scotland. *Working for patients.* London: HMSO, 1989. (Cmnd 555.)
2 Secretaries of State for Social Services, Wales, Northern Ireland, and Scotland. *Promoting better health.* London: HMSO, 1987. (Cmnd 249.)
3 Secretaries of State for Social Services, Wales, Northern Ireland, and Scotland. *Primary health care: an agenda for discussion.* London: HMSO, 1986. (Cmnd 9771.)
4 Wilkin D, Metcalfe DHH. List size and patient contact in general medical practice. *Br Med J* 1984;289:1501-5.
5 Fleming DM, Lawrence MSTA, Cross KW. List size, screening methods and other characteristics of practices in relation to preventive care. *Br Med J* 1985;291:869-72.
6 Morrell DC, Evans ME, Morris RW, Roland MO. The "five minute" consultation: effect of time constraint on clinical content and patient satisfaction. *Br Med J* 1988;292:870-3.
7 Royal College of General Practitioners. *The classification and analysis of general practice data.* 2nd ed. London: RCGP, 1986.
8 British Medical Association and The Pharmaceutical Society of Great Britain. *British national formulary.* London: BMA and Pharmaceutical Press, 1987.
9 Cartwright A, Anderson R. *General practice revisited.* London: Tavistock, 1981.

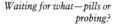

Waiting for what—pills or probing?

CRISPIN HUGHES, PHOTO CO-OP

A GP's perspective

Andrew Harris

Despite the increased choice for mobile patients offered by the plans in the white paper there are two dangers: the withering of the community services and the inadequacy of the core services where the district health authority uses non-local hospitals. Increasing the capitation element of general practitioner pay is retrogressive, as are the target payments for procedures such as immunisation and cervical cytology. Real difficulties will arise if large group practices begin to operate their own budgets, and patients' nagging doubts that budgeting considerations played a part in their doctors' decisions represent a totally unacceptable alteration of a professional relationship.

The flaw in the white paper is that though the NHS review was set up as a result of political pressure about the NHS cash crisis, it produces no new funds.[1] But pleas for increased funding or protests about the hidden agenda of future privatisation, although justifiable, will be ineffectual. Mr Kenneth Clarke said in the Commons, "We shall, of course, listen particularly to the views of the public and the patients." He will not be negotiating with the medical profession for agreement, only to discuss operational details. The question now is, "Will the government's reforms improve services and choices to patients or not?" We should welcome some of the managerial and efficiency reforms but highlight our concerns for patient care by urging our patients to speak out.

The proposal for tax relief on private health insurance for the over 60s—even if taken out by a relative—coupled with the Prime Minister's remark that those who can pay for themselves should not take up the beds of others, is a clear indication that Mrs Thatcher views the NHS of the future as a safety net rather than a comprehensive service for all. Comprehensive cover for the over 60s with BUPA is about £2900 a year, an amount few can afford. Retired people who have such means should not be made to feel guilty about using the NHS nor should they need to consider private care if the government's proposals for an internal market are successful. In a Gallup poll published in February 56% of pensioners were against the tax relief proposals intended for them, and I believe we should encourage them and organisations such as Age Concern to voice loud consumer protest.

Fundamental changes eclipsed

So much attention has been focused on the opportunity for hospitals to become self governing trusts that the fundamental changes in funding and provision of all health authority services has been eclipsed. Health authorities will be funded for the populations they serve, hospitals will be funded according to the services they provide, and general practitioners will be free to refer out of the district with the patient's own district health authority paying the hospital that the general practitioner chooses. While this will create increased choice for mobile patients who are not acutely ill, there are two dangers. Firstly, community health services for the chronically ill and elderly will wither. Secondly, the core services to which patients need to be guaranteed local access by the district health authority will be inadequate where the district health authority elects to use non-local hospitals for some services. I doubt that there will be many hospitals that opt to be independent trusts. While in the short term they will offer a competitive stimulus to improve services in surrounding hospitals, especially in London, tight restraints are needed to prevent them from concentrating on profitable forms of health care to the detriment of the community.

With the internal market pressures towards efficiency savings how will health authorities ensure that hospitals provide the less marketable services such as domiciliary physiotherapy, district nursing, health visiting, occupational therapy, and community psychiatric nursing without a deterioration in standards of care? Mrs Thatcher's distaste for local government led to the sidetracking of the Griffiths proposals for community care, and the lack of a response from the government puts a big question over the future of community care. The only clue I can find in this white paper is the bringing of family practitioner committees under regional health authority control, and a sentence, "Larger districts might eventually become candidates for mergers with family practitioner committees." Is this a prelude to moving community health services to a budget, shared with general practice, under family practitioner committee control?

> "... I suspect that practice budgets will become an insidious way of commercialising primary health care."

If we are to ensure that we do not return to pre-1948 days when funding a health service was seen as funding a hospital service the government must chart a way forwards for care in the community, including personal social services, public sector housing, and rehabilitation services. With general practitioners and local authority members losing their representation on health authorities, we should press for a mechanism of local accountability. Just as directors are answerable to their shareholders at the annual general meeting, so should health authority members be answerable to patients and general practitioners in the area, perhaps by an annual report to community health councils.

London SE22 0QR
Andrew Harris, MRCP,
general practitioner

Correspondence to:
77 Underhill Road, London
SE22 0QR.

Br Med J 1989;**298**:884-5

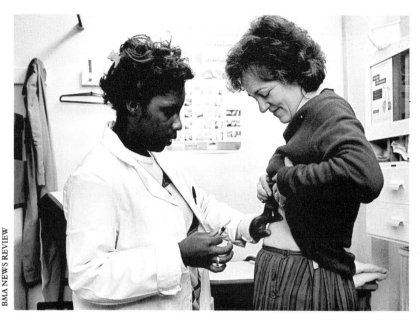

Will the practice be able to afford the nurse?

The government's commitment to increasing the capitation element of general practitioner pay is retrogressive. In some areas it will lead to shorter consultations and longer waits, although its effect might be softened if there was a much larger weighting for elderly patients. It is important that practices with large lists that seek to recruit nurse practitioners or extra administrative staff are not prevented from doing so by cash limiting of the ancillary staff budget. More serious is Mr Clarke's stated intention to replace item of service payments with target payments for childhood immunisation (90%) and cervical cytology (80%). This is potentially damaging to inner city practices, where the rapid turnover of socioeconomically deprived patients will prevent attainment of these targets, thus establishing a disincentive for such activities. Despite the promise of special help for inner city practices made by the government in *Promoting Better Health* we still await the financial details.[2]

The development of prescribing information systems into indicative drug budgets for general practitioners is an important and useful source of information, which in future will be provided for every general practice. Provided that the budgets are set to take into account individuals who need regular appliances and highly expensive drugs such as growth hormone, immunosuppressives, drugs for anaemia in renal dialysis, and antiviral and AIDS agents, they should not be feared.

The difficulties of budgets

Real difficulties will develop for all practices if large group practices begin to operate their own budgets:

- Even the most organised of practices will need an enormous increase in management and administrative staff, premises improvement, investment in high technology, and training of the primary care team

- Despite the promise of a management fee for those practices operating a budget it is unclear where the resources will come from or how the budgets can be fairly set
- If practices with budgets are able to increase their income and offer extra services, such as their own physiotherapist and minor surgery, two tier general practice will inevitably develop
- Market forces may make small practices relatively uneconomic and thus more scarce
- Consumer choice will be limited and the scheme will sound the death knell for the best of traditional small general practice, where the doctors' knowledge of the families on their list probably outweighs the advantages of any information system
- The inclusion of drugs in the practice budget will present difficult ethical problems because for the first time a doctor's choice of drug for a patient will have a direct effect on the practice income.

Even more worrying is that despite the Secretary of State's reassurances[3] some practices with budgets will find it financially prudent not to register chronically ill or disabled people or frail elderly people, as their consumption of health care may be viewed as an unacceptable financial burden. Patients needing referral for investigation or treatment may not feel confident that they are being offered the best advice—particularly at the end of the financial year—as they will have that nagging doubt that the budgeting considerations of their doctor played a part. This is a totally unacceptable alteration of a professional relationship, quite out of keeping with the traditions of British, or indeed much European, practice. Furthermore, it creates a position where there is an incentive for the general practitioner to refer his patients privately.

I suspect that practice budgets will become an insidious way of commercialising primary health care. None of the reassurances of Mr Clarke that there are ways of auditing practice accounts and giving financial incentives to practices, to prevent professional standards from suffering, are convincing. General practitioners who want to opt for their own budget are either greedy or naive. It is essential that patients—particularly in large group practices—make their views known to their doctor.

This white paper skilfully transfers responsibility for obtaining or providing services on to the shoulders of general practitioners without extra government money for patient care. So when there is an outcry in the future about underfunding the health service the government will point the blame at the managers and doctors. General practitioners don't want to be part of Mrs Thatcher's political agenda, but unless the patients' views are voiced independently of the medical profession and party politics, and doctors refrain from defending their illusory clinical freedom, all our misgivings will be ignored.

1 Secretaries of State for Health, Wales, Northern Ireland, and Scotland. *Working for patients.* London: HMSO, 1989. (Cmnd 555.)
2 Secretaries of State for Social Services, Wales, Northern Ireland, and Scotland. *Promoting better health.* London: HMSO, 1987. (Cmnd 249.)
3 Warden J. MPs' question time on NHS review. *Br Med J* 1989;**298**:481.

30

Self governing hospitals

Ray Robinson

The freedom of self governing hospitals to fix rates of pay may help in attracting good quality staff, at the possible expense of neighbouring NHS hospitals. It may also reduce the volume of services that can be provided, given that costs will no longer be contained by the monopoly power of the government. The second freedom, for self governing hospitals to manage their own capital stock, should lead to the first consideration of the relative costs of capital and labour—but at the risk of a heavy impact of these costs on hospitals occupying expensive inner city sites. Audit will be an important element in maintaining the quality of service, and, although a two tier system of hospitals is unlikely, there may well be threats to comprehensive local provision at the margins.

The devolution of decision making to the local operational level is one of the government's main objectives for the NHS. This is expected to secure local commitment; to produce services that are more responsive to the needs of patients; and to achieve greater value for money.[1] Encouraging the establishment of self governing hospitals is a key component of the policy designed to meet these aims.

Self governing hospitals will operate as independent trusts within the NHS. Each trust will be run by a board of directors with the chairman appointed by the Secretary of State. The board will be responsible for determining overall policy, while day to day management will be the responsibility of the general manager. Trusts will derive their income from service contracts obtained from district health authorities, general practitioner budget holders, and private patients. The government views competition between trusts, other NHS hospitals, and private hospitals as a mechanism for increasing efficiency and patient choice.

Initially it is intended that trusts will be restricted to major short stay hospitals with over 250 beds, although eventually other hospitals are expected to become eligible for self governing status.

- The government has a flexible definition of a self governing hospital

- Self governing hospitals could offer a range of community based services as well as acute care

- There could be self governing community units

- Neighbouring hospitals offering complementary services could combine into a single self governing unit.

Most of the advantages expected to result from self government derive from the greater autonomy that hospitals will be given to manage their own affairs. As in the case of the government's privatisation programme greater freedom from centrally imposed restrictions and bureaucratic control is expected to improve management's performance. Two main areas where this will apply are employment policy and capital spending.

King's Fund Institute, London NW1 7NF
Ray Robinson, MSCECON, *health policy analyst*

Br Med J 1989;**298**:819-21

Employment policy

Self governing hospitals will be given the freedom to determine their own staffing levels, rates of pay, and conditions of service. This freedom will cover all categories of staff, including doctors and nurses. The white paper argues that it is particularly important that trusts should be able directly to employ their own consultants. In determining rates of pay they may find it convenient to adopt national agreements. Alternatively, they may opt for arrangements that suit their local labour market conditions. Clearly, the government intends to remove what it sees as restrictive practices on pay and employment and to encourage a far more competitive labour market. What consequences can be expected to result from these changes?

Freedom to determine rates of pay will almost certainly result in the emergence of wage and salary differentials between hospitals. Hospitals that are successful in competition for service contracts will be able to offer higher rates of pay to attract good quality staff. Similarly, hospitals located in areas with tight labour markets will have more freedom to offer competitive wages and salaries. In some cases, of course, higher rates of pay will lead to higher unit costs and place hospitals at a relative disadvantage when bidding for service contracts. In other cases improvements in productivity at more efficient hospitals can be expected to offset higher rates of pay.

The ability to determine their own rates of pay will offer more flexibility and may work to the advantage of self governing hospitals, but it could have deleterious effects on staff recruitment and retention at other NHS hospitals. Nursing staff, for example, might be expected to respond to opportunities to earn better salaries in self governing hospitals, especially if salaries in other hospitals continue to be restricted by national pay agreements. Some NHS hospitals are already suffering from the loss of key nursing staff to the private sector in specialties such as intensive care and theatre nursing. Competition from self governing hospitals may well exacerbate this type of problem.

> *". . . doctors can also expect to be affected by the emergence of salary differentials."*

Doctors can also expect to be affected by the emergence of salary differentials. Apart from variations in rates of pay between hospitals there may well be greater variation within hospitals. Some specialties will hold more revenue generating potential than others. In a system of workload funding there will be an incentive to link salaries more closely to the income generated by individual doctors and specialties. How far and fast this process will develop is difficult to predict.

Similar uncertainties surround changes in conditions of service. The government intends that existing staff in hospitals that become self governing will have their present conditions of service protected. But this will constitute a major restriction on management's freedom over employment policy. As such there will be clear advantages in maximising the rate at which new staff contracts are implemented. These are likely to be of fixed term duration. Indeed, instead of employing consultants directly there may be attractions in employing them on a subcontracted basis for defined workloads.

In addition to its impact on pay differentials greater freedom for individual hospitals to determine their rates of pay may also exert upward pressure on overall NHS spending levels.[2] One of the great merits of the NHS—which became increasingly apparent to ministers during the review preceding the white paper—is its ability to contain total spending. Unlike most other countries the United Kingdom does not suffer from overall cost inflation. Far from it: according to many people costs are contained too effectively. A major reason for successful cost containment has been the monopoly power of the government as a purchaser of health service labour. If hospital trusts are given freedom to determine their own rates of pay this monopoly will be eroded. Of course, the government will still be able to control total spending via the public expenditure planning process. But it will become susceptible to new pressures. Generally wage drift—that is, payments above nationally agreed rates—results in increased spending because higher earnings are not offset by reductions elsewhere. Moreover, some districts will find that they face higher prices for services from their local self governing hospitals—as a result of its higher salary levels—and that without adequate allowance for this price inflation in their cash allocations there will be a reduction in the volume of services that they are able to buy. This can be expected to be yet another source of calls for increased funding.

Capital spending

The other main freedom which is to be offered to self governing hospitals is the freedom to manage their capital stock. Trusts will be given the power to acquire and dispose of assets. They will be able to borrow funds for investment purposes either from the government or from private institutions, although this power will be subject to an annual financing limit. And they will be able to make operating surpluses that can be used to finance future investment projects. These additional freedoms—together with the decision to introduce a system of capital charges into the NHS—offer the scope for a more rational approach to capital decision making. Management attention will be focused on the use made of the NHS's substantial holdings of estate and capital assets. It should lead for the first time to consideration of the relative costs of capital and labour and to a more thorough examination of their appropriate mix in providing services.

Set against these advantages there must be reservations about the impact of capital charges on those hospitals occupying expensive, inner city sites—especially in London—and the extent to which limits on aggregate spending determined by the Treasury will continue to restrict managerial freedom.[3]

Quality of service

Self government will offer hospitals greater freedom to determine their own objectives. Constraints on their activity will arise from various government imposed regulations and the need to attract service contracts within a competitive market. The government expects the latter constraint to encourage the cost effective provision of services as rival hospitals seek to offer competitive prices. There is always a danger, however, that efforts to control costs will lead to reductions in service quality. Market competition—where purchasers have only fixed budgets to spend—poses a

The resource management initiative hospitals, such as Huddersfield Royal Infirmary, hold the key to how self governing hospitals might work—yet the government will not wait for the results

particular threat. Interestingly, competition in the United States has had precisely the opposite effect. Research evidence suggests that it has led to an increase in quality.[4] But this is because in the absence of effective control on total costs hospitals have competed in terms of quality instead of price. Cash limits are likely to prevent this state of affairs occurring in the NHS.

The possibility that service quality may be jeopardised by competition makes the government's decision to strengthen medical audit especially important. It is envisaged that by April 1991 each district health authority will have established a medical audit advisory committee. These will be chaired by a senior clinician and include representatives from the major specialties

---

"... many hospitals now seem more cautious about applying for self governing status as the pitfalls become more apparent."

---

and general management. The committees will have a variety of functions including the production of annual reports. These will identify clinical performance over the previous year and point to areas where action is needed to improve quality or efficiency in the future.

The proposal to strengthen and extend systems of medical audit has generally been welcomed. But questions still persist as to whether it will be sufficient on its own to ensure acceptable standards in the new competitive environment. Audit is a system of peer review. It is, in essence, self regulation by the providers of health care. Many people, including the National Association of Health Authorities,[5] are unhappy with this. They have argued that monitoring should be carried out by an independent body such as an accreditation agency or an NHS inspectorate. Ministers, however, have rejected these suggestions.

Local service provision

Self governing hospitals are expected to secure local commitment and to offer services that are more responsive to their patients' needs. Yet concerns have been expressed that they may sever links with the local community and undermine attempts to provide a comprehensive range of services for local patients. The spectre has been raised of glamorous teaching hospitals offering high technology medicine to a national or international clientele while the needs of the local population suffering from chronic sickness are

neglected. In fact, the white paper states quite clearly that core services will have to be provided locally to guarantee local access. Community based services, including those for elderly or mentally ill people, are mentioned as examples of these services. It is unlikely that the Secretary of State would permit a self governing hospital to refuse to enter into a service contract for the provision of such services if there was no adequate alternative in the locality.

Claims that hospital trusts will mean a reversion to the pre-1948, two tier system of voluntary and local authority hospitals are surely exaggerated. None the less, there may well be threats to comprehensive local provision at the margins. When decisions about the most cost effective or profitable use of individual beds are made by managers financial considerations may well provide incentives that act against the interests of some non-remunerative local services. To avoid this danger monitoring should extend beyond clinical outcomes and incorporate more general data on the comprehensiveness of services and access to them.

Conclusion

Self governing hospitals will represent an untried form of organisation operating within an untested market environment. It is impossible to say with any certainty how they or the market will perform. This will become clear only if and when the new style NHS gets under way. Recognition of the uncertainty surrounding these and other proposals led to widespread calls for experiments in the period of debate leading up to the publication of the white paper. But ministers have rejected this option. The white paper is about implementation not experimentation. Fortunately, however, the conditions that the government has specified as a prerequisite for attaining self governing status will mean that the pace of implementation can be only gradual. Indeed, after much initial enthusiasm many hospitals now seem more cautious about applying for self governing status as the pitfalls become more apparent. Present indications suggest that there is unlikely to be a rush of volunteers. All of this should mean that the process of implementation will at least provide the opportunity to learn by doing and to adjust the model of a hospital trust as its strengths and weaknesses become apparent.

1 Secretaries of State for Health, Wales, Northern Ireland, and Scotland. *Self governing hospitals. Working paper 1*. London: HMSO, 1989.
2 Barr N, Glennester H, Le Grand J. *Working for patients? The right approach?* London: London School of Economics, 1989.
3 Robinson R. New health care market. *Br Med J* 1989;298:437-9.
4 Pauly M. Efficiency, equity and costs in the US health care system. In: *American health care: what are the lessons for Britain?* London: Institute of Economic Affairs, 1989.
5 National Association of Health Authorities. *Working for patients. NAHA's response to the House of Commons Social Services Committee*. Birmingham: NAHA, 1989.

Doubtful gains from tighter consultant contracts

W J Appleyard

The advantages of independence for hospitals include raising money and developing services faster. The disadvantages may be the provision of only limited services and too rigid a contract, making extra, unpaid, clinical work, teaching juniors and students, and administrative time much less attractive. The loss of consultant goodwill would outweigh any supposed advantages of the new system.

Dr W J Appleyard was interviewed by Dr Tony Smith on the working paper on consultant contracts and distinction awards. Dr Appleyard is a member and former deputy chairman of the Central Committee for Hospital Medical Services.

Let's talk first about the sensitive matter of contracts. Consultants are worried on two counts: who will really control their contracts and how flexible these will be in form and in daily operation.

We are told that as the trust hospitals evolve consultants' contracts are going to be held by these hospitals and not by the regional health authority. Traditionally, NHS contracts have been held at the regional level (except for the university and postgraduate teaching hospitals). So in some ways the trust hospital might follow the pattern of the university hospital.

The advantage of contracts being held at region in terms of consultant work is that most of the specialist services that consultants provide are confined to one district. True, general medical and surgical services may be based in a single district, but most subspecialties are provided on a multidistrict basis and have a regional structure.

Increasingly, the pattern of patient services is of primary care by general practitioners, referral to the secondary consultant care service—in the hospital and in the community for the maternity, paediatric, psychiatric, and geriatric services—and then a further layer of tertiary care for the subspecialties and for those topics that require more intensive research in teaching centres. It is important to plan those services both nationally and regionally. If we allow the growth of trust hospitals to be totally independent and based on market forces any planning will be extremely difficult to sustain. The new trust hospitals may not be interested in the difficult cases, and they may be more concerned in getting rid of their waiting lists as a political or as a financial objective.

There are, however, certain advantages in independence—for example, for raising money and developing some services faster. But the risk is that the trust hospital may decide to offer only limited services. In recent years we have seen some important and cost effective changes in the integration of secondary care services within the community and the hospital. One example is geriatric services; the consultant geriatrician must be appointed to the district—not just a hospital—and run the community sector as well. Mental health is the same. And of course in paediatrics we have for far too long been inefficient, keeping two service arms—the child health service and hospital paediatrics—

Kent and Canterbury Hospital, Canterbury, Kent CT1 3NG
W J Appleyard, FRCP, consultant paediatrician

Br Med J 1989;298:739-41

though we are now moving towards integration. It is not spelt out in the white paper whether trust hospitals may take on these services and if so how. And if they take some bits on and not others that would create a disorganised service. It is also difficult to see what incentive would be provided for a trust hospital to keep beds available for emergencies. Currently we are being asked in the south east region to keep our intensive care beds filled 100% of the time. Now that is absolutely impossible to do in any acute service.

Until now the regional status of consultant contracts has meant two things: firstly, we have had good specialist services, and, secondly, the specialists have been prepared to work outside the big teaching centres. One important feature of the health service has been its even spread throughout the country. If we come to have just a few trust hospitals which concentrate skills we might destroy that concept of overall service.

Experienced staff

Another point about the contracts being held at regional level—a system, incidentally that Alain Enthoven supported—is that regions have staff who are able to cope with such complexities as complaints by patients, and so on. Ideally, I believe that contracts should stay at regional level, but some aspects could be delegated to the district. Of course, to some extent that happens now, with the district deciding the content of the contract and seeking approval from the region. One more important safeguard is that it is desirable professionally that a contract is overseen by the royal colleges and the universities so they should be represented on the appointments committees. We would certainly wish that system to continue in order to guarantee the high standard that is required of the consultant grade.

The government is proposing that the general manager should be on the advisory appointments committee. These are important meetings for deciding distinction and overall professional competence of the candidate. Usually all the candidates are well qualified, and it is a question of sorting out with local interests what special talents might bring to the post. Now if we

---

"... a London trust hospital could say, 'We are going to pay you half the amount because you are bound to earn a lot in private practice.'"

---

are going to require a major input of management skills that might militate against the care of patients. Existing appointments committees comprise seven people, one of whom is a representative of the district health authority. We would prefer to have any management

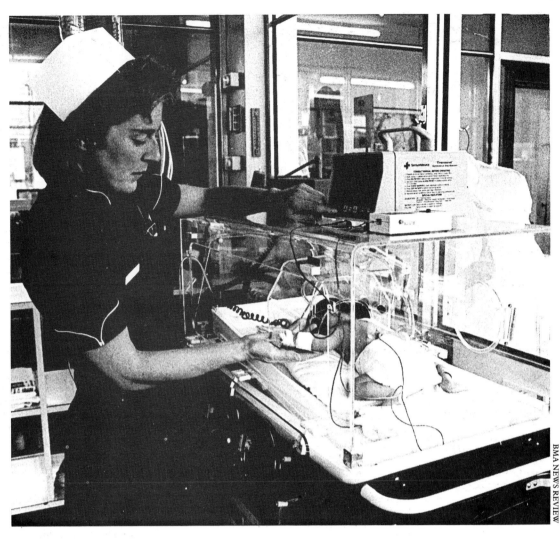

What does 24 hour responsibility mean?

input at that level rather than from the chair. Clearly in future some further training in management will be part of the consultant's education. I believe that the existing training teaches them to manage rather well; we shall have to look carefully at what other elements they are going to have to learn. But we shall also want to know what criteria the manager on an appointments committee would apply to the candidate. Furthermore, we should insist on being on the appointments committees as managers to ensure that they will command the profession's confidence.

Job descriptions

The existing job descriptions were agreed about 1979 as part of the new package with the then Secretary of State for Social Services, Patrick Jenkin. One important element was the concept of whole time and maximum part time. Under both contracts the consultants devoted substantially the whole of their time to their NHS tasks. There is a list of duties that we have—the diagnosis and treatment of patients at one or more hospitals, domiciliary consultations, and so on—as well as a continuing clinical responsibility for patients in our charge allowing for proper delegation to and training of the staff. The white paper puts it about that we have 24 hour responsibility. That concept is open to considerable misinterpretation. I think we have continuing clinical responsibility for the patients in our charge, but not for any new patients arriving at the hospital unless we are on the duty rota. We do have continuing responsibility for those people in our care but we can delegate that responsibility to colleagues. This is how it works in custom and practice, and I

would not want that to change. The patients know which consultant is looking after them and who is responsible for their care.

The building brick of the consultant contract is the notional half day and this will apply in any future negotiations. This is a three and a half hour period of time flexibly worked and aggregated up to a total of 35 hours for 10 notional half days a week. The key aspect, however, is its flexibility, so that these are not sessions requiring a consultant to be in at 9 o'clock precisely—just as you wouldn't expect a manager to be at his desk at any particular time because his duties may call him away elsewhere.

I come in at around 8 15 am and visit our special care baby unit before I go on to the clinic. So my time of arrival at the clinic is determined by the emergencies that have come in overnight. Of course it is entirely reasonable that a consultant should be expected to be there to run a clinic when everybody is geared up to it. But some of the work is variable, and on a knock for knock basis I think that the health service has gained a considerable amount over the years from this flexible working pattern. A survey carried out by the Office of Manpower Economics showed that consultants were giving the NHS up to 25% extra work above their contracted sessions.

A too rigid contract will work against patients

The concern is that if the new system defines the contract too rigidly it will actually work against the interests of patients. Should the government enclose and encapsulate the doctors' work much more rigidly than now a lot of that extra work is not going to be done unless the health authority pays for it. Certainly there are few doctors who don't fulfil their contract satisfactorily; they are a small minority who are relatively easily identified. When consultants are collectively responsible for running a unit and one of them is just not discharging these responsibilities then the best way to deal with the problem is to sit round a table and the backslider can be shamed in front of the others.

> *". . . the consultant is in everyday contact with patients. This is the big difference between the consultant and the manager."*

The existing job description also includes provision for teaching. We are responsible by custom and practice for teaching the juniors who work for us; that responsibility we enjoy. Any attempt to formalise that more clearly will mean identifiable time will have to be set aside. If it is then formalised as part of our 35 hour week of course it will mean that the service will have to have more consultants doing the other clinical duties. At present many consultants regularly take on students—on monthly and sometimes two weekly rotations. That work is totally unrecognised, but increasingly it will be a necessary part of the students' education because the central hospitals are just not going to have the range of patients they need for teaching students. If this sort of teaching is recognised it will be a bonus for the district hospital. It won't be a bonus for the teaching hospital, however, because part of its budget will be redistributed.

More staff

One other thing about the job description; we have been careful not to box people into their job description and designation of duties simply because the nature of a consultant's work is flexible. I never know when I go into a hospital exactly what will happen that day, everything is totally unpredictable in terms of clinical demands. If audit is introduced we shall all need to have a session or so put aside—perhaps more than the initial one or two sessions—for managing the clinical service and auditing it. So more time will be taken away

from patients in that way. Overall more staff will be needed to get through the clinical workload if teaching, audit, management, and those other elements that the government has rightly identified are to go ahead.

I would like to see a basic contract of 10 notional half days which could be built on, so that the more work you did for the health service the less work you could do in private practice. And I am sure it is right that we must have systems which provide a guarantee to the managers that if you are contracted for a particular amount of work you actually do that amount. But outside those duties you should be able to contract to do other things. Consultants working just for the health service would be able to contract extra sessions for their administrative work, their teaching duties, and so on, building on that contract. It would be helpful for the trust hospitals to have a basic, nationally agreed contract on which they could build to suit local needs.

Pay bargains

I would be very worried indeed if a trust hospital was free to adjust the nationally agreed basic contract. For instance, in London a trust hospital could say, "We will pay you only half the usual amount because you are bound to earn a lot in private practice." So Guy's Hospital might pay only half the salary offered at Canterbury. The other worry about giving a contract to the trust hospital is the fact that the consultant would then be entirely in the hands of the local general manager. General managers are transient beings. Their objectives may be short term, whereas the evolution of a specialist service is inevitably a long term objective. There could be a clash between the consultant trying to build up and develop services over the long term and the general manager who is trying to meet certain short term fiscal targets.

Nowadays when there is such a clash the general manager can't simply say "you're fired" or "we don't need you any more" because he has to go through the regional health authority to do so. But in future he may be able to fire a consultant at whim. And if a consultant is under contract to a trust hospital rather than the region and the trust hospital went broke because, say, of bad management he would lose his job instead of being redeployed. So there may be considerable disadvantages in locally negotiated contracts, mainly arising, I think, from the transient nature of managers and the longer term perspective of consultants.

Finally and crucially, the consultant is in everyday contact with patients. This is the big difference between the consultant and the manager. He sees and he touches and he talks to them, and he's the frontline guy. I know he's supported by junior staff but he's still seeing patients face to face—a real safeguard for them. If the doctor thinks the service is inadequate or in difficulties he knows this from first hand experience and can speak out without fear of being rapped over the knuckles by his manager.

An alternative to distinction awards

Now let us move on to distinction awards. Traditionally they were to reward distinction. Over the past 10 years meritorious service awards crept in. More and more of the B and C awards are being given to people who have borne the heat and burden of the day. My personal view is that I've always found it difficult to be comfortable in a system that gives awards to over 60% of consultants and not to the others. I think that in any system you can always identify the top 10% who are quite outstanding, and probably you could always

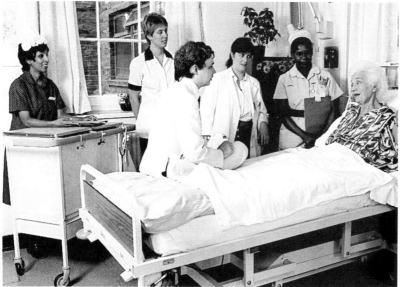

Teaching is currently unrecognised work for many consultants. A new contract may mean specific time allocated to teaching—and less time to spend on other things

JULIA MARTIN, PHOTO CO-OP

identify the bottom 10%. But to make arbitrary distinctions within the other 80% has always been a fatal flaw in the system.

A while ago the idea was floated that we should have a seniority payment after 10 years of service in the health service. That would mean an award slightly lower than the C award but recognising long service. The service could redistribute the existing awards money to fund a long service award and on top of that you could have far fewer distinction awards for the truly outstanding consultant. The white paper is proposing a move towards managers having a much greater say in the selection of people for distinction awards, because the health authorities are actually paying the money.

I notice that the trust hospitals are going to pay for the awards for their consultants. That will affect some of their budget decisions. So long as awards are given for consultants' outstanding abilities and research and various national activities that they have performed I think it is quite wrong to require an individual hospital to foot the bill. At present, too, there is an element of equalisation—trying to achieve a reasonable proportion in all the specialties, but unfortunately not all specialties attract doctors with the same degree of merit. That is a fundamental flaw. Under the new system all proposals for awards will have to go through a general management scrutiny first and then there will be a professional decision. Reading between the lines, I think that is what the government wants. If, however, there is to be a real distinction award system for professional merit I don't think that the general manager should have an input into that. And looking back to my comments on the importance of consultants being able to criticise the service provided for their patients, if management has a filtering effect on distinction awards consultants are going to be less likely to speak out on the patients' behalf. But essentially I don't see how a manager could really comment on anything but a consultant's management abilities. If an awards committee wishes to give somebody a justifiable award for research or other professional work I fail to see how the manager can contribute to that judgment. So I come back to my view that we should have seniority payments, which of course managers could influence, with on top of those a few purely professional distinction awards.

Finally, who will pay for consultants attending committees in the new structure? At present if we are representing our colleagues we get payment through an agreement with the Department of Health. The same applies to attendance at royal college meetings or the General Medical Council. Our contracts allow us to do this because of their flexibility; we can make arrangements to see people at alternative times or delegate to juniors and pick up the bits when we come back. The white paper's proposals mean that regional activities of royal colleges will be enhanced and so require more of the profession's time. At present we have an informal knock for knock basis. From the personal point of view I've had difficulties attending some of the Department of Health's information advisory group activities and I've made it quite clear that unless a locum was funded I couldn't attend. And that was accepted.

I said at the start that contracts are a sensitive issue for consultants. If the government and health authorities impose closely monitored inflexible contracts the consequences may well be that consultants will look carefully at how much extra unrewarded work they do for the NHS not just in the wards and outpatients but also in the many advisory and representative committees to which they contribute. Any loss of consultant good will or sense of responsibility as a result of government changes would outweigh any supposed advantages of more tightly controlled contracts.

Internal markets for surgical services

Richard J Fordham, Raymond J Newman

Demand for acute and elective orthopaedics is so high that internal markets between districts are likely to be established early — and the policy is likely to be welcomed by the public. Finance will follow patients and successful hospitals will thrive — while the less successful ones may contract and even cease to exist. Careful pricing policies will be necessary, together with some allowance for unforeseen complications. Nevertheless, the market is unstable and regulation will be necessary to maintain the public interest.

This paper is based on discussions held at a recent conference for general managers in the Yorkshire Regional Health Authority on developments arising from the NHS review. The innovation of internal health service markets — that is, trade in medical and surgical workload between health authorities — was considered and the clinical and economic consequences of such markets for orthopaedic surgery in particular were examined.[1]

The white paper *Working for Patients* represents the cumulative achievement of the most radical free market proposals for the NHS since the government came into office in 1979.[2] Change has occurred in a step wise fashion through several measures designed to alter the cultural norms of the health service. Increased local accountability, quicker decision making,[3] the identification of key decision makers,[4] contracting out of non-clinical services, cost improvement schemes, and efficiency through the resource management initiative have all played a part in preparing the NHS for these latest reforms. The government has stopped short, however, of full privatisation in the face of continued overwhelming public and professional support for a tax based, zero priced health care system.[5]

The NHS review has instead introduced several free market principles, such as greater consumer sovereignty and increased competition among producers, while remaining within a state run framework. Greater choice and diversity of services in primary and secondary care are to be encouraged, with value for money and efficient use of resources being the ultimate goals.

Health Economics Consortium, University of York, York YO1 5DD
Richard J Fordham, MA, *research fellow*

St James's University Hospital, Leeds LS9 7TF
Raymond J Newman, FRCS, *honorary consultant orthopaedic surgeon*

Correspondence to: Mr R J Newman, St James's University Hospital, Beckett Street, Leeds LS9 7TF.

Br Med J 1989;298:882-4

> **". . . elective orthopaedic surgery lends itself to the internal market."**

District health authorities will become the procurers rather than providers of the most cost effective health provision for their population. The larger general practices will be able to shop around on behalf of patients for the services they require from the hospitals of their choice. Similarly, enterprising hospitals will be able to extend their role to the provision of services for a wider population unconstrained by arbitrary administrative boundaries. The cash following the patients is to be the new NHS maxim lending greater financial flexibility to health care delivery than could ever be envisaged (or coped with) under the rules of the Resources Allocation Working Party formula.[6]

Implications for orthopaedic surgery

Orthopaedic departments will be fundamentally affected by the proposed changes and particularly by the concept of trade between districts. Trade may occur between units in different authorities as well as directly between orthopaedic surgeons and general practitioners. These trading relationships are known as internal markets and will affect both the so called core hospital services outlined in the review — for example, accident and emergency — as well as other hospital services — for example, elective surgery. The volume of demand for both acute and elective orthopaedic surgery is such that we can expect to see the early establishment of such trading.

Elective orthopaedic surgery lends itself to the internal market business. Waiting lists and waiting times vary greatly between districts while the most common surgical procedures required are small in number and similar in most hospitals. The procedures and outcomes are generally well defined and trade in this area will be seen by hospital authorities as a means of getting more out of existing resources, improving efficiency, and reducing waiting lists. It is also a policy that will probably win public support because it may be seen as a potential panacea for perhaps the biggest shortcoming within the NHS — long waiting lists for non-urgent conditions. Under what circumstances will trade take place and what are the practical difficulties?

There are several reasons why orthopaedic units may wish to trade with one another, but the primary reason is likely to be profit or the generation of additional revenue for the seller and savings for the buyer. At the margins of current output some districts may find themselves with the capacity to handle extra cases at little additional cost while charging their customers a price nearer to average cost. As for the buyers some authorities will want to purchase procedures outside their district at the given market price because they can be supplied more cheaply than undertaking them in house. Others may have different incentives to trade such as constraints on local capacity and pressure to cut waiting lists. Profit may not be the only reason for trade and entrepreneurs may have subsidiary goals — for example, to utilise spare capacity in order to retain economies of scale, to attract recognition for training, and to acquire grants to finance costly research.

Historical precedent

From an economic point of view there is a historical precedent dating back at least to Adam Smith's *Wealth of Nations* in 1776, which supports the theory that free trade leads to better allocative efficiency of national resources than can be achieved under a command or heavily regulated economy.[7] Neoclassical economic theory has strongly influenced all Western economic policies, interrupted only by the post-war Keynsian interventionist era (during which the NHS was created). Vilfredo Pareto's theory that optimal social allocation of resources could be derived only by independently motivated consumers and producers exchanging goods and services in the market has dominated Conservative thinking on social welfare policy since the early part of this century.[8]

The main irony of the market as Adam Smith himself pointed out is that it is inherently unstable. Left to their own devices producers tend to collude against the public interest to attain even higher profits and greater market share. Nearly every market for a particular good therefore requires some form of regulation. There may be several reasons for this—for example, to prevent customer exploitation, improve consumer sovereignty, or ameliorate the side effects of undesirable productive activities on society. In some markets the scale of production required is so large and barriers to entry become so formidable that a single producer becomes a natural monopoly. In such cases there is little economic evidence as yet that current policy of deregulating these public enterprises promotes greater efficiency.[9] It is early days yet for this policy in the NHS but much will depend on how and in what spheres competition is introduced. A sensible approach even for the most risk taking hospital would be the introduction of trade on a specialty by specialty basis, monitoring carefully the results of pilot projects.

Internal markets in orthopaedics may initially be restricted to low priority, high volume cases such as minor elective surgery. Subsequently, this may be extended to a trade in sophisticated and specialised procedures which are in the mutual interests of both parties to undertake. Nevertheless, in a more highly deregulated market some hospitals will wish to adopt a more aggressive outlook, undercutting their competitors, reinvesting profits as a means of growth, and expanding productive capacity to reap economies of scale. Units that start with an advantage in size, facilities, and skills are likely to do even better under these reforms. They may also pay higher wages to attract high quality staff by taking advantage of the new regulations on pay and conditions. The decline or extinction of orthopaedics in the range of specialties we have come to expect from most health authorities may even occur as workload is concentrated in fewer centres.

Trade is a two way contract and needs to be considered both from the buyers' and sellers' points of view.

Buyers' point of view

Whatever incentive there may be for buying orthopaedic services the procurers must firstly decide how much they have to spend and what types of surgical procedure are required. Do they want to buy minor or major procedures or achieve a particular balance of case mix? This will depend on the buyers' priorities— for example, are they trying to maximise a reduction in the size of waiting lists, in waiting times, or expenditure? They must also consider that contracting, say, all minor cases may leave their departments with an imbalance of major workload or vice versa. This will have subsequent effects on their own theatres and bed utilisation requirements. Other management responsibilities for the clinicians will be to ascertain much more specifically than may be known at present how much in house services cost for comparative procedures—particularly if greater efficiency is the overriding objective.

In purchasing orthopaedic services from another district or from the private sector health authorities will be concerned with ensuring acceptable standards of surgery and care that must at least meet those of their own department. Again this may not be as straightforward as it seems. To do this objectively requires a detailed audit of in house performance including assessments of operative mortality and morbidity and longer term results. The latter may be relatively easy to decide for minor procedures but for total joint replacement five or even 10 year follow up data are required to assess the success or failure of the operation. In order to achieve a regular standard of quality of care it may be necessary to ensure suitability of patients by careful preselection in terms of age group, general health, and stage of the disease process requiring surgery.

Patients' preferences also need to be considered. An

Adam Smith: fons et origo

". . . the days of the local hospital having a natural monopoly are numbered."

---

agreement between two authorities 250 miles apart, although financially attractive to the hospitals concerned, may not be so convenient for the patient or the ambulance services. It will also impose substantial extra costs on patients in terms of travel, time off work, etc, not reflected in the officially agreed price.

There are two other important clinical considerations requiring attention by the purchaser. Firstly, how and for how long will patients be followed up after their operations? Will a formal contract stipulate whether this will be undertaken by the supplier or the originating orthopaedic department? Follow up will probably have to be split into immediate postoperative assessment and longer term review, particularly for major operations. Secondly, what would be the seniority of the surgeon performing the proposed procedure? Would it be an experienced consultant or a registrar in training and who would determine this? If the latter was the case would all hospitals be eligible to sell services or only those recognised by the Joint Committee for Higher Surgical Training?

Direct trade between health authorities, especially for elective surgery, may also require consultation with those general practitioners who have not negotiated their own arrangements with a particular hospital. Named referral will obviously be affected by this practice. It may also conflict with the wishes of those general practitioners holding practice budgets who will want to use the hospital departments of their choice.

Sellers' points of view

Those hospitals who see themselves as suppliers of treatment in these new markets will need to develop careful pricing policies. If the suppliers are charging a fixed price per operation in any one period (it will of course fluctuate in the longer term) the major incentive for them will be to minimise costs in order to maximise profit. We hope that because of professional standards this would not jeopardise quality of care but this will need to be monitored routinely both by supplier and purchaser.

Methods of minimising costs when setting a price are to place conditions on the selection of patients or to levy additional charges for unanticipated complications requiring extra care. These precautions minimise the risk of reducing profit or even making a loss by the supplier. Fortunately, the incentive to reduce risk also falls on the buyer who will not wish to incur undue complications in subcontracted patients and who will want to minimise expenditure. But surgery is a high risk business and some allowance for the completely unforeseen complication needs to be made when the supplier is fixing prices. Similarly, should a factor be incorporated for complications which may appear many years after the surgery—for example, low grade sepsis in a total joint replacement? American health insurance organisations who use diagnostic related groups to reimburse hospitals for treatment for standard conditions are trying to overcome the problem of deviation from the mean by more specific definitions of patient groups. Although not a complete solution to the problem, the corollary of internal markets might be the widespread introduction of a diagnostic related group system to enable better pricing and to control costs.[10]

The effect on nursing resources of selling substantial numbers of operations must also be considered since these patients will have to be cared for in addition to local patients being treated simultaneously. This review would have to take place both at the ward and community levels. Hospitals which accept further workload will have to use existing establishments cautiously as many already suffer from low morale and staff shortages. Higher pay might attract additional good quality staff and help to retain existing staff.

Finally, what medicolegal obligations would the sellers assume? Would they be totally responsible or would part of this responsibility still be borne by the buyer? Subcontracting of patients would at least require a legally binding contract specifically setting out these responsibilities. This would be an appropriate role for regional health authorities in addition to the negotiation and administration of contracts.

Challenging times ahead

The NHS review will instigate a radical new free market climate in our health care system. It espouses the principles of consumer choice and value for money. Hospitals are to be encouraged to seek the most cost effective services available and will be free to offer services to their own and other districts in order to attract funds. Finance will follow patients and successful hospitals will thrive while there is a possibility that less successful ones will contract and even cease to exist.

The days of the local hospital having a natural monopoly on the provision of services to its population are numbered, even if that hospital does not chose to opt out of administrative control by the district. Hospitals and individual clinical departments will therefore depend to a varying extent on attracting business from wherever it may be found. In specialties such as orthopaedics where the demand for elective surgery is high fierce competition may be expected. How smaller district general hospitals will fare against their larger teaching hospital rivals remains to be seen. Competition between hospitals of similar size may take the form of price or non-price wars, with departments offering either a cheaper operation or one performed more quickly.

Though the discussion has been directed at orthopaedic surgery the same considerations apply equally to all medical and surgical specialties. When hospital departments begin to trade in internal markets they will be obliged to consider their position as buyer or seller of services (or both in some cases). They will have to face problems, such as the definition of product, pricing, constraints, clinical and legal responsibility, risk, etc.

We thank the Yorkshire Regional Health Authority; the Nuffield Institute of Health Service Management, University of Leeds; and the Health Economics Consortium, University of York, for arranging the day conference on internal markets, and we are grateful to the members of the group who discussed the implications for orthopaedic services and who shared their ideas with us. The views expressed here are the personal views of the authors.

1 Akehurst R, Brazier J, Normand C. *Internal markets in the National Health Service: a review of the economic issues.* York: Centre for Health Economics, University of York, 1988. (Discussion paper No 40.)
2 Secretaries of State for Health, Wales, Northern Ireland, and Scotland. *Working for patients.* London: HMSO, 1989. (Cmnd 555.)
3 Department of Health and Social Security and Welsh Office. *Patients first.* London: HMSO, 1979.
4 NHS Management Inquiry. *Report.* London: DHSS, 1983. (Griffiths report.)
5 Jowell R, Witherspoon S, Brook L, eds. *British social attitudes.* London: Social and Community Planning Research Unit (Gower), 1987.
6 Department of Health and Social Security. *Sharing resources for health in England. Report of the Resource Allocation Working Party.* London: HMSO, 1976.
7 Smith A. *The wealth of nations, 1776.* London: Pelican, 1977.
8 Pareto V. *Manuel d'économie politique.* Paris: Girard and Brière, 1909.
9 Kay JA, Thompson DJ. Privatisation: a policy in search of a rationale. *Economic Journal* 1986;96:18-32.
10 Havigust C, Helms R, Bladen C, Pauly M. *American health care—what are the lessons for Britain?* London: Institute of Economic Affairs, 1989.

JCC's evidence to social services committee

Sir Anthony Grabham, chairman of the Joint Consultants Committee, gave oral evidence to the House of Commons social services committee on 5 April on behalf of the committee, which represents all doctors in the NHS on matters other than pay and terms of service. He was accompanied by Sir Ian Todd, president of the Royal College of Surgeons, Mr A P J Ross, CCHMS chairman, and Dr Graeme McDonald, HJSC chairman.

Br Med J 1989;**298**:1090-1

Aims of the white paper

The Joint Consultants Committee strongly supports the aims set out in the Prime Minister's foreword to the government's white paper *Working for Patients*.[1] It believes, however, that the means put forward in the white paper to achieve these aims need very careful assessment to ascertain whether they are practicable, desirable, or appropriate.

Principles

The review is based on an underlying principle that competition, in the shape of market forces, increases efficiency and increased efficiency releases resources. It presupposes this must allow a better standard of treatment or more treatment within the same level of resource. The general validity of this principle in the world of business is not questioned.

The proposals brought forward now have been drawn from a variety of sources in different countries. In some instances the original concepts are still experimental and in others they have already failed. The committee will need to be convinced that the application of these proposals is compatible with a National Health Service which uniquely aims to provide universal equity of care. Encouragement of many NHS hospitals to become self governing, for general practices to have practice budgets, for district health authorities to be purchasers of health care rather than providers—all of which will mean some hospitals "succeeding" and others "failing"—will interfere with the proper planning of this equitable provision of care for the community as a whole.

The proposals and the implied expansion of competition are also dependent on accurate costing. Currently it is generally accepted that the level of management information in the health service is woefully inadequate. The JCC has collaborated with the Department of Health in the establishment of six resource management pilot schemes, which have proved expensive and of limited success to date and are not yet properly evaluated. Indeed the JCC and the NHS Management Board had already agreed on the necessity for and the timetable of a programme of evaluation. On present information, however, the JCC seriously questions whether it will be feasible to introduce the information technology needed to provide the facts, on which the competition must be based, within the timescale suggested. Accurate costings cannot be generally available for at least several years and will be enormously expensive to introduce throughout the health service. It will involve both acquiring the appropriate computer systems needed for the NHS and also recruiting the skilled staff needed to install and modify the systems to suit the varying demands of individual hospitals. To introduce such an expensive and wide ranging reorganisation before the resource management initiatives have been adequately evaluated is bad management.

Detail

Very little detailed information is in fact available, so reference will be made only to some of the very many proposals put forward.

PROPOSALS TO CREATE SELF GOVERNING HOSPITALS

These proposals inevitably change the prime aim of the management of these hospitals from the provision of adequate care to the community as a whole to the financial success of the hospital. The considerable experience of such hospitals in the United States shows clearly that there will be pressure to encourage admission of patients with conditions that can be treated with financial benefit to the hospital rather than to admit those patients—often the chronic sick—whose treatment is likely to lead to little or no such financial benefit. The organisational costs of hospitals in the United States exceeds 15% of the budget in comparison with around 5% in the NHS; they therefore spend proportionately much less on direct patient care. Moreover, the service to patients—particularly the poor and the chronic sick—falls far short of the comprehensive service available under the NHS.

The JCC is concerned, too, about the absence of adequate mechanisms to ensure the maintenance of standards in self governing hospitals. The profession has cooperated with the Department of Health at national level in working out solutions to problems which can then be implemented throughout the whole of the health service. Complaints procedures, management of private practice, data protection, discharge of patients, and the waiting lists initiative are recent examples of detailed discussions which have resulted in helpful improvements throughout the service. Under the new proposals there would be no method of ensuring that guidance on issues agreed nationally would be implemented in self governing hospitals.

The absence of a clear commitment to the continued implementation of centrally agreed medical manpower policies is a matter of particular concern to the JCC, which has worked closely with the government to draw up the detailed strategy set out in *Achieving a Balance*[2] and *Plan for Action*.[3]

Finally, the committee believes that the abandonment of a national remuneration structure for hospital doctors might increase salaries for some doctors, but none the less would be a retrograde step and is not consistent with the long standing principle of uniform standards throughout the country. An even spread of the best consultants, both geographically and by specialty, has been essential in maintaining equality of access to health services. It was for precisely this reason the Spens Committee recommended in 1948 that a national remuneration structure be adopted for consultants. The introduction of market forces would damage gravely this principle.

FUNDING AND CONTRACTS FOR HOSPITAL SERVICES

The aim of relating hospital funding more directly to the work done is welcomed. However, any proposed system for achieving this needs to be considered carefully. If some hospitals are encouraged to attract more patients and therefore more funds, within a global total, it follows that the funding of some other hospitals will suffer. The budgets of the "losing" hospitals could well fall below the critical mass necessary to sustain core services in their own areas. Furthermore, there needs to be a more specific national definition of core services, with greater emphasis on the elderly, the chronically sick, and the mentally ill. The fixed price contract funding mechanism suggested is untried in the context of the National Health Service and will clearly limit patient choice. The documents suggest that the final decision on referral of a patient to another hospital for treatment will depend more on the managerial and financial considerations rather than the patient's wishes and a medical assessment of clinical needs.

PRACTICE BUDGETS FOR GENERAL MEDICAL PRACTITIONERS

The JCC, composed of hospital doctors, will deal with this proposal only briefly. Its main concern, however, is that the trust between the doctor and the patient might be impaired when the patient knows that the doctor's decision on his treatment might be directly influenced by the doctor's limited budget or by prior contractual arrangements with a particular hospital. In addition, hospitals may have a weakened incentive if practice budget holders retain any savings that accrue from increased hospital efficiency—given that the hospital services elements of such budgets are to be derived by regional health authorities from the hospital and community health services allocation. At present comparable savings arising from increased hospital efficiency can be used by the hospital itself to improve its services elsewhere.

CAPITAL CHARGES

The proposals are interesting but could well be impracticable, because the effect on patient care is far from certain. The committee is seeking more information on these proposals.

MEDICAL AUDIT

In recent years the profession initiated and has been increasingly involved in medical audit, particularly through the royal medical colleges and faculties, and it will continue to be so. A major extension of audit, however, requires good information systems, and the committee welcomes the government's recognition that it will be very expensive in terms both of time and of money. It hopes this money will be provided separately and not be taken from existing resources for patient care.

MEDICAL EDUCATION AND RESEARCH

The white paper contains few direct references to medical education or research. The major changes that will occur, however, when the white paper is introduced may have serious deleterious effects on both of these subjects and very much more detail is required. There is little reassurance that the present support for medical education at all levels in NHS hospitals will be maintained in self governing hospitals or that the present facilities—for example, postgraduate medical centres—will continue to be supported. The careful medical manpower planning of hospital posts for postgraduate training may be jeopardised by the need for self governing hospitals to put their own priorities before those of national requirements.

The JCC questions whether the environment that allows clinical and laboratory research to take place will be maintained or that the new initiative will be allowed to develop when the emphasis is on patient costing rather than care for a community. For example, it doubts whether pain clinics or the new hip replacement operation, both developed by research within the NHS, would have occurred had the new system with its financial imperatives been in place.

The interface between academic and NHS medicine is extremely important to both sides—for undergraduate and postgraduate education, and for both basic and applied medicine; it is essential that the universities and the royal medical colleges and faculties are given adequate time for full consultation on the complex issues involved.

Consequences of failure

If this scheme is to be introduced throughout the service in essentially its present form some thought must be given to the consequences of complete or partial failure. If, as the JCC fears, the information systems are simply not able to provide the accurate information needed within the timescale suggested then there will be a prolonged period of great uncertainty and confusion in the health service. If inaccurate estimates are substituted for accurate costing information then hospital planning and the service to the community will be greatly distorted. Furthermore, some of the proposals must mean a substantial increase in organisational costs without any corresponding improvement in patient care. Indeed, unless the total NHS budget is increased substantially there would be a significant reduction in the resources available for the treatment of patients. It is essential, therefore, that a careful evaluation of pilot studies is undertaken before a more widespread implementation of these proposals. It should be noted that such studies were in fact proposed in Alain Enthoven's monograph on the management of the National Health Service—a document seminal to the white paper itself.[4] The JCC believes that a failure to test these proposals in practice before their general introduction will inevitably be shown to be a major error of judgment.

1 Secretaries of State for Health, Wales, Northern Ireland, and Scotland. *Working for patients.* London: HMSO, 1989. (Cmnd 555.)
2 Department of Health and Social Security, Joint Consultants Committee, chairmen of regional health authorities. *Hospital medical staffing: achieving a balance.* London: DHSS, 1986.
3 Department of Health and Social Security, Joint Consultants Committee, chairmen of regional health authorities. *Hospital medical staffing: achieving a balance: plan for action.* London: DHSS, 1987.
4 Enthoven A. *Reflections on the management of the National Health Service.* London: Nuffield Provincial Hospitals Trust, 1985.

Distinction and merit awards— a £100m management tool?

James Raftery

Based on suggestions made in the 1988 report of the review body the white paper's proposals on merit awards emphasise that these should benefit the NHS as well as individuals, should have an age limit, and should be subject to review with greater management input. The original objectives of merit awards have little relevance today. By changing to reflect commitment to service management as well as clinical excellence merit awards should pull clinicians further into management—a further step in the transformation of medicine in the United Kingdom from administration to management.

The system of distinction and merit awards, which grew out of an agreement in 1948 between Aneurin Bevan and Lord Moran, president of the Royal College of Physicians, has survived with few changes for the 40 years up to the recent NHS review.[1]

The white paper proposes that discussions should begin with the medical profession with the following changes in mind:

• To modify the criteria for C awards so that in future consultants must show not only their clinical skills but also a commitment to the development and management of the service
• To restrict progression of the remaining three levels of awards to those who have earned C awards
• To change the composition of the regional committees which nominate candidates for C awards. In future, each committee will be chaired by the regional health authority chairman and will include senior managers as well as clinicians
• To change the composition of the national Advisory Committee on Distinction Awards to provide for stronger management influence on the choice of award holders
• To make the new or increased awards reviewable every five years
• To make new or increased awards pensionable only if a consultant continues working in the NHS for at least three years

The brief, 11 page working paper provides details on some of the organisational changes envisaged— namely, that nominations for C awards would be expected to have the support of both clinicians and management and that membership of the Advisory Committee on Distinction Awards be supplemented by a senior person with experience of NHS management.[2] Thus, management will have a veto on the nominations for C awards as well as a greater input to the allocation of higher awards.

Criticisms of the merit awards

The system of distinction and merit awards has recently received considerable attention with the publication of the first detailed description of its working[3] and questions in parliament about the cost of the system. The House of Commons social services select committee, which suggested in 1983 that major change in the distinction awards might be salutary, has announced its plans to review the award system.

From its beginnings the award system has been controversial. It was seen in 1950 by the Treasury as a "blot on the landscape of public finance," which was accepted only on the grounds that "arguments of expediency outweigh those of principle."[4] Extraordinary secrecy surrounded the awards, with the first limited information about the distribution of awards by specialty becoming available only in 1958 in response to parliamentary questions. Secrecy and the uneven distribution of awards by specialty, region, and sex have been the main subjects of subsequent criticism.

In a series of articles two of the more persistent critics concluded that the system should be abolished

> "... the continuation of merit awards on top of locally determined salaries in the NHS trusts seems anomalous."

because "it remains immutably unfair, divisive and, in its secrecy, contemptible. No other profession would copy this system and consultants would gain respect by scrapping it—especially self respect."[5-7] Other critics have echoed these points in more temperate language.

The first official criticism of the awards scheme emerged in 1988, when the review body on doctors' and dentists' remuneration, having expressed concern that the awards should benefit the NHS as well as reward individuals, suggested that awards should have an age limit and be subject to review with a greater managerial input into the selection process. The working paper on merit awards makes it clear that the white paper's proposals are based largely on these suggestions.

Objectives of the award system

Five objectives of the award system have been outlined:
• To reward outstanding individual distinction
• To attract the highest calibre entrants to the medical profession
• To provide earnings comparable with the highest in other professions
• To provide a means of attracting consultants away from the major teaching centres
• To compensate consultants for loss of private practice.

Only the first objective retains contemporary relevance.

Department of Clinical Epidemiology and Social Medicine, St George's Hospital Medical School, London SW17 0RE
James Raftery, MA, *lecturer in health economics*

Br Med J 1989;**298**:946-8

Aneurin Bevan and Lord Moran came to an agreement on merit awards in 1948; Bevan said later that he had stuffed the consultants' mouths with gold. Clarke would like to spend merit award money differently

REWARDING DISTINCTION

Since most consultants take up their positions by the time they are 40 some form of incentive for continuing professional commitment seems appropriate. The key question concerns who should apply what criteria in allocating awards. Hitherto, the medical profession has been left to decide on the allocation of the awards in private, with neither the public nor general practitioners allowed to know who has an award. Indeed, other consultants were allowed only from 1979 to know who held awards and then only in their region.

The proposed changes in the system redefine "meritorious service and distinction" to include performance in a management context. At present district managers have indirect influence only on C awards through their regional chairmen, who can make recommendations to the regional committees. Regional committee membership has, until now, been confined to the profession and selected by existing award holders. In future these committees will be chaired by regional health authority chairmen and include several senior managers. This enhanced role of managers goes hand in hand with the proposal to provide defined job descriptions for hospital consultants, which will be reviewed annually, with management monitoring whether they are being met. Merit awards, by changing to reflect "commitment to service management as well as clinical excellence," will pull clinicians further into management, a process initiated by Sir Roy Griffiths 1983 report.[8] That report led to the appointment of district and unit managers on short term defined contracts with salary scales comparable to consultants, plus performance related pay increments of up to 30%. The white paper, which was produced by a team which included Sir Roy Griffiths, extends the management approach to clinicians. Merit awards will become a type of performance related pay.

None of the other stated objectives seems relevant today. Recruitment to medicine can hardly have been affected by merit awards since they were so confidential. While merit awards undoubtedly raise medical salaries, this objective could and is being achieved in other ways—for example, through private practice and potentially through locally negotiated salaries in the NHS trust hospitals. Estimated consultants' private earnings at over £300m in 1987[9] exceeded the total cost

---

"... recruitment can hardly have been affected by merit awards since they were so confidential."

---

of merit awards of just under £100m (see below). Merit awards, far from being used to disperse consultants away from the major teaching hospitals as envisaged by the 1948 Spens report, may have contributed to the opposite effect as the chance of earning awards was greatest in certain major centres and specialties.[4] Compensation for loss of private earnings, which may have been relevant in the founding of the NHS, has little relevance today when private practice is no longer frowned on by the government.

Costs

As many of the original objectives of merit awards have lost much of their relevance costs have risen as the awards have come to be used to supplement pensions. Seniority plays a large part in the allocation of awards, as shown by the fact that while only 36% of consultants on average hold awards at any one time, 70% do so by the time they retire. Superannuation is paid to consultants on the basis of final salary including merit awards. Since employees' superannuation contributions cover only a small part of the cost of pensions extra costs are imposed on the state by retired award holders. The total cost of the award scheme thus includes both revenue costs of current award holders and the increased, unfunded, superannuation payments to retired award holders.

Revenue costs of distinction and merit awards

	No of awards				Value (£m)				Authorised budget (£m)	Amount paid out* (£m)
	A+	A	B	C	A+	A	B	C		
1 4 1980	141	523	1498	3450	17·4	13·34	7·95	3·53	33·5	28·9
1 4 1981	144	532	1525	3511	18·62	14·34	8·59	3·83	36·9	31·8
1 4 1982	144	532	1565	3601	19·645	15·13	9·06	4·04	39·6	34·2
1 4 1983	147	542	1595	3750	20·825	16·04	9·605	4·28	43·1	37·2
1 4 1984	150	554	1631	3750	22·39	17·24	10·33	4·6	47·0	40·6
1 4 1985	162	602	1649	3792	27·3	21·02	12·01	5·35	57·2	49·3
1 4 1986	162	652	1679	3852	27·3	21·02	12·01	5·35	58·9	50·8
1 4 1987	182	652	1679	3902	29·55	22·75	13·0	5·79	64·6	55·8
1 4 1988	192	692	1679	3902	33·72	24·85	14·2	6·26	71·9	63·4

*This is obtained by adjusting the authorised budget by 86·3% for the years to 1987 and by 88·1% in 1988.

REVENUE COSTS

The revenue costs of the award system can be readily estimated from the reports of the review body on doctors' and dentists' remuneration. Each year's report contains data on the number of awards by type and the value of each type. Combining the numbers of award holders and the values of each type of award gives a first estimate of the revenue costs (see table). But as the review body has noted not all award holders are employed full time. The notional "authorised budget" overestimates spending as some award holders receive reduced awards because they work part time or hold honorary contracts. Although no central information is available on the numbers whose salaries and awards are thus reduced, the Department of Health estimates that 86% of the authorised total was paid out in the years to 1987 and 88% in 1988.

The results of these calculations put the revenue costs of the award system at £56·9m in 1987 and £63·3m in 1988. Both the number of consultants holding awards and the value of the awards have increased in recent years, but the percentage of eligible consultants holding awards has remained unchanged at close to 36%. Distinction and merit awards thus account for a fairly stable 4% share of the medical revenue budget and some 10% to 15% of all consultant salaries (based on the extremes of the consultant salary range).

SUPERANNUATION COSTS

Although detailed information on the superannuation costs of the award system is not available, these can also be estimated. The number of retired award holders can be calculated using an average life expectancy for those retiring of 14 years and an average of 500 retiring each year.[11] Combined with official estimates of the notional pension contributions necessary to finance merit awards, the total superannuation cost comes to £39.9m in 1987. Thus the total cost of the award system, comes to just under £100m in 1987, £57m being direct revenue costs and £40m superannuation costs. Previous estimates, which have ignored the superannuation costs, have seriously underestimated the real cost of the award system.

Conclusions

The white paper proposes to change the definition of merit and widen the award allocation process to include management. Hitherto, consultants made awards to their peers on criteria which were ill defined and primarily clinical. In future, awards will be made by management and clinicians on criteria related to job descriptions and services delivered. Although consultants' contracts will continue to be held by regional health authorities, they will be managed by districts who will have much greater say in the appointment and monitoring of consultants.

Hospital consultants will be moved towards a clinical version of performance related pay similar to that of managers. These proposals can be seen as the extension of the shift to a management culture in the NHS introduced by the Griffiths report on general management. The proposed changes will be achieved by threat and inducement: the threat being provided by means of the annual review of individual contractual obligations and the inducement being that of enhanced pay, whether through merit awards or higher salaries in NHS trust hospitals.

The rationale for nationally agreed merit awards combined with locally negotiated pay, however, remains unclear. The majority of larger hospitals that will be encouraged to become NHS trusts will control their own salary levels, including those of consultants. The continuation of merit awards, set at national levels, on top of locally determined salaries in the NHS trusts seems anomalous.

A judgment on the desirability of further incorporating clinicians in management depends on your view of the contemporary role of medicine. Much depends on whether and to what degree doctors respond to financial incentives and whether medicine can be managed.

The attempt to manage medicine and health services has spawned several new subdisciplines such as health economics and health policy studies. Experience elsewhere, particularly in the United States, suggests that considerable progress can be made in categorising, quantifying, and managing what goes on within the black box labelled "clinical freedom." Tighter definitions of cases, such as diagnostic related groups, are already part of the resource management initiative that the white paper is building on. Similarly, the increased interest in measurement of outcomes by cost effectiveness studies and quality assisted life years signals future trends. Research is also proceeding in the United States on methods of remunerating doctors on the basis of human and physical resources required in carrying out certain procedures by means of resource based relative values, which implies that payment rates should vary by specialty.[12]

Recognition of both the increased power and limitations of medical interventions, combined with demands for greater individual choice and responsibility, plus increased concern over costs, all point to a widespread trend in favour of stronger management of health services. Since hospital consultants play a key role in making decisions it is difficult to see how they could remain aloof. Whether clinical freedom is alive or dead, what happens in the clinic will increasingly be judged by criteria which transcend the purely clinical.[13] The proposed changes in the merit award system mark but one further step in the transformation of medicine in the United Kingdom from the era of administration to management of health services.

1 Secretaries of State for Health, Wales, Northern Ireland, and Scotland. *Working for patients.* London: HMSO, 1989. (Cmnd 555.)
2 Secretaries of State for Health, Wales, Northern Ireland, and Scotland. *NHS consultants: appointments, contracts and distinction awards. Working paper 7.* London: HMSO, 1989.
3 Edwards B, Pennington GW. *Distinction and meritorious awards for hospital doctors and dentists in the NHS.* Keele: University of Keele, Health Services Manpower Review, 1987.
4 Webster C. *The health services since the war: problems of health care, the National Health Service before 1957.* London: HMSO, 1988.
5 Bruggen P, Bourne S. The distinction awards system in England and Wales 1980. *Br Med J* 1982;284:1577-80.
6 Bourne S, Bruggen P. Secrecy and distinction. *Br Med J* 1987;295:393.
7 Bourne S, Bruggen P. Re-examination of the distinction awards in England and Wales, 1976: the new advisory committees. *Br Med J* 1978;i:456-7.
8 NHS Management Inquiry. *Report.* London: DHSS, 1983. (Griffiths report.)
9 Laing W. *Laing's review of private healthcare 1988/89.* London: Laing and Buisson, 1988.
10 Interdepartmental Committee in the Remuneration of Consultants and Specialists. *Report.* London: HMSO, 1948.
11 Department of Health and Social Security. *Hospital medical staffing: achieving a balance: plan for action.* London: HMSO, 1987
12 Hsiao W, Braun P, Becker ER, De Nicola M, Ketcham TR. Results and policy implications of the resource-based relative value study. *N Engl J Med* 1988;319:881-8.
13 Williams A. Health economics: the end of clinical freedom? *Br Med J* 1988;297:1183-6.

Welcome for medical audit

Walter van't Hoff

Audit should not be restricted to care within the resources available: clinicians need to point out where these are inadequate. Other worrying aspects of the white paper proposals include a concentration on quantity rather than quality (however difficult this is to assess), the inclusion of medical members on audit committees representing the district general manager, and the possibility of initiating independent audit—giving rise to an adversarial relationship. Any analysis will need accurate data, which will not be provided by implementing the Körner report. Despite these reservations, however, audit will gradually become accepted by the profession, particularly as an educational rather than a harshly critical exercise.

Dr Walter van't Hoff was interviewed by Dr Tony Smith on medical audit. In 1979 the physicians at the North Staffordshire Hospital Centre, where Dr van't Hoff worked, introduced medical audit, and in 1985 a medical audit committee was established covering all specialties.

Stone, Staffordshire
ST15 8DP
Walter van't Hoff, FRCP, former consultant physician

Correspondence to:
Greylock, Airdale Road, Stone, Staffordshire ST15 8DP.

Br Med J 1989;298:1021-3

Much of what the working paper on medical audit says will be welcomed by the profession.[1] Indeed, it reflects much of what most of the royal colleges have been introducing in the past few years—and particularly in the recent report of the Royal College of Physicians, a report which I helped to prepare.[2]

I have, however, some reservations and some doubts. Firstly, I wonder whether the meaning of medical audit to the Department of Health is the same as to the professions. On the first page of the working paper the definition of medical audit is one that doctors wouldn't argue with. Medical audit is described "as the systematic, critical analysis of the quality of medical care, including the procedures used for diagnosis and treatment, the use of resources, and the resulting outcome and quality of life for the patient." But further on it says that an effective programme of audit will help to provide the necessary reassurance to doctors, patients (I would prefer to put patients first but never mind), and managers that the best quality of service is being achieved within the resources available.

Now it is, of course, the duty and responsibility of doctors when doing medical audit to point out any particular aspect where resources are inadequate. I don't think we should be restricted in our thoughts to the resources that are currently available, for we all know there are many features of the NHS with inadequate resources, and this is something that we need to point out.

Furthermore, there are two sorts of resources—money and manpower. Certainly it comes within our remit to consider whether it is proper use of a doctor's time, for instance, to do cervical screening every year when the time might be better employed doing other things.

Indeed, this is one of the problems of medical audit generally—doctors could spend so long auditing themselves or other people that there would no longer be time to do the work that they are really meant to be doing. The obvious solution is to pick on a few aspects that obviously need looking at, home in on those, and examine them in detail. We cannot possibly look at everything in the time available.

Taking advice

We are also told that the government wishes to work with the profession in addressing issues of medical audit and it has recently asked the Standing Medical Advisory Committee to consider and report on this. I'm just a little concerned, however, that this committee may be too Whitehall oriented. I would be happier if the government had approached all the colleges and so obtained the views of all specialties. And although the government has introduced a central fund to support medical audit, it is really quite small (£250 000). To do medical audit properly needs the time not only of clinicians but also of records departments, of secretaries, and of finance departments in order to be able to get accurate recall of information. Obviously that means computers, so the amount of money that is on offer is going to seem extremely small.

Another worrying aspect is that the government seems to be going to concentrate on numbers of patients treated rather than on what is actually done to them. I can easily see twice as many outpatients in a clinic as I have done in the past, but somebody needs to make a judgment on whether that is good for the patients or just good for my numbers. This is where the great difference may well lie between the profession and the government; doctors are primarily concerned with quality and I have a feeling that the government is primarily concerned with quantity, though that is not actually spelt out in the white paper.

Quality is, however, extremely difficult to assess—especially when you turn from specialties such as obstetrics or surgery or pathology, in which quantity and quality are comparatively easy to assess, to the more difficult specialties such as medicine, general practice, and psychiatry. Here quality of care is paramount and quantity often less important. Deaths and disasters are easily measured outcomes. But if we are to look at outcomes in terms of successes then the question to be posed is who measures the quality of the outcome—is it the clinician, or the patient, or perhaps the patient's relatives? They might have three quite different views on the outcome of treatment. Take the treatment of hypertension. The patient's blood pressure may come down but he or she may feel terrible and quite unable to get out of a chair. Or the patient may simply not feel fit to go to work. And I think these things must also be taken into account when assessing results.

Patient satisfaction alone is, however, something I am wary of. I know examples of doctors whose practice has not been of the highest quality as judged by their colleagues but whose patients have been delighted with the way they have been looked after. Whether or not the patients are really much better is difficult to say, but the fact that they are pleased with the treatment they have received is an important factor. So we have to

The Royal College of Physicians has given a recent boost to medical audit, emphasising its educational role

If we do not train any of our junior staff on the job there will be no experienced staff in the future to take our places. The only question is the degree of back up that should be available and how easy it should be for the more junior doctors to get in touch with their senior colleagues should they require help. But for junior members of staff to be left alone without the facility for getting advice or practical help should the need arise is, however, a matter of concern.

Yet another disquieting phrase in the working paper is the reference to "initiating independent audit." If a manager is concerned about a certain part of the service he or she is fully justified in pointing this out to the audit committee and asking whether the matter needs to be looked into. But if the manager initiates an outside audit this becomes extremely adversarial and would be looked on with great misgiving by all doctors. Such outside audit should be done only in extreme circumstances—for instance, when the audit committee has refused to look into something that the

---

". . . many of the procedures that are numerically satisfactory are not always the best for the patient."

---

manager believed was a grossly irresponsible action by a clinician, such as introducing a controversial procedure that was prohibitively expensive.

The small specialties have a particular problem because there might well be only one or two consultants in that specialty in a particular district. And obviously they would have much greater difficulty than their colleagues in, say, general surgery in comparing their results with each other. Here a wider or more regional audit such as has been done in Scotland would be sensible—and the working paper suggests that. But it also suggests that the proposed regional audit committee should not only have a representative from each district but also have them chosen to ensure that all the main specialty interests are covered. That seems to be wanting to cover everything. I'm not sure what such a regional committee with representatives from each district is going to do except to say that they are doing medical audit and in their view they are doing it satisfactorily. More realistically, in many regions there are subcommittees of specialties and these subcommittees could well be asked whether they would be responsible for audit in their particular specialty throughout the region. I don't see any need to have a new committee because many of us spend more than enough time in committees already.

weigh up the two factors, patient satisfaction on the one hand and the actual results in clinical terms on the other. And this is difficult. We must not forget, as I said earlier, that audit is a time consuming business. It could not be done for all procedures by all doctors on all patients. The only practical way is to tackle particular problems that could produce benefits.

Audit committees

My next cause for concern is the suggestion that audit committees should have as members "doctors representing the district general manager." I believe that these doctors' prime loyalty would be to the general manager rather than to their colleagues, and this is something that many clinicians would view with some suspicion. In any case many doctors still view clinical audit with apprehension, and it is not universally welcomed, although attitudes are changing fast. But how far the district general manager should be concerned in audit is a cause for real worry.

Clearly if a medical audit showed evidence of a severe deficiency of one sort or another then it would be the manager's responsibility to be aware of this. That may well be, but in order to talk freely at medical audit meetings it has always been assumed that confidentiality covers patients and doctors. And I would prefer in the first place that general managers or their representatives were not present at medical audit meetings. But if a gross deficiency was discovered the chairman of the medical audit committee or the chairman of the relevant specialty committee would then need to speak to whoever was clinically concerned. If that approach produced no satisfactory response the clinician might then be invited to discuss the problem with a group of peers such as the "three wise men." Only if that procedure failed should the managers be brought in.

Technical competence

Studies looking at technical competence have commonly shown, for example, that surgeons in training don't perform as well as fully trained consultants. Making those sorts of results routinely available to the managers might cause a lot of disquiet within an audit committee. Indeed, there is currently widespread concern that there may be moves for all surgery to be done by experienced surgeons and all outpatients to be seen only by consultants and not by doctors in training. I think that this is a naive concept.

Quality of care

My particular interest in medical audit has always been the quality of medicine in so far as it affects the patient and the quality of patient care. And this is something which perhaps the managers might be a little less interested in than, for instance, the overall number of operations performed and the number of one type of operation compared with the number of another type. Some of the white paper is couched in terms that sound as if they might well have come from the private health companies; and the less dramatic specialties, the ones where numerical factors are more difficult to use, particularly geriatrics and psychiatry, are hardly mentioned. For example, one paragraph in the working paper suggests that "the relevant parts both of the forward programme and the annual report should be made available to other health authorities considering placing contracts within the district." It seems to me that the government would like us to move from medical audit in terms of patient care into medical audit as a form of advertising. This is certainly not what most of the profession has in mind when it talks about medical audit.

Many of the procedures that are numerically satisfactory are not always the best for the patient. It might well be that the patient who is discharged early may take longer to get back to work than the one who is kept in hospital another two or three days. So we need to look a lot further and deeper than in terms of figures and lengths of admission and so on. Such calculations are also muddled by the extremely inaccurate information that we have been getting to date as a result of the implementation of the Körner reports, which were supposed to improve the NHS's information systems. Unfortunately, if we are not careful it is these figures that are going to be used for making decisions.

Fewer referrals equals better care?

Another aspect of this obsession with numbers is the apparent assumption by the health departments that the general practitioner who refers comparatively few patients to outpatients is providing better care than his or her colleague who refers a larger number. Presumably they will finish up by calculating a sort of norm and saying that this is the right thing to do. But the general practitioners who refer few patients may be extremely bad or they may be extremely good in that they do many of their own investigations and use the diagnostic facilities available to them. In our hospital we have found that only about a third of general practitioners regularly use the pathology and radiology services, which are open to all of them. The remainder find it easier to refer patients to an outpatient clinic.

The problem with norms is that in cold surgery, for instance, most patients take the same course, assuming that they have no complications, but for medical conditions, pneumonia for instance, there are so many variables—the severity of the pneumonia, the age of the patient, how fit or unfit the patient was before developing the pneumonia—that any norm would end up as a fairly meaningless figure. Different parts of the country, too, would have different types of patients and different types of care that would affect this. We cannot eliminate the variations in a problem with so many facets as illness and it would be naive to try to do so. We hope that medical audit will provide an opportunity to look at these problems, and if, for instance, it was found that in a particular district or region patients spent much longer in hospital than in others some inquiry would make sense. It might well be found, however, that there were completely logical and sensible explanations.

Persuasion of the reluctant

We are moving into a new era in which audit is not going to be a purely voluntary process on the part of doctors. Certainly the recent Royal College of Physicians' report has emphasised the educational aspects of medical audit in terms of teaching people to accept audit and to make it a constructive rather than a harshly critical exercise. We can all improve our practice and one of the things that doctors need to do is to accept a more open attitude to what they do and to be willing to discuss the management of patients with their colleagues. And if that management has in any way been imperfect we need to learn from the exercise.

Some apprehension among some doctors exists even in those hospitals where medical audit has been running for some years. Now if medical audit is to become a necessary part of medical practice everybody will need to take part. But I do think that gradually doctors will accept that it is normal for their professional practices to be discussed by their colleagues. Certainly junior staff accept this more readily than some of the older clinicians, which is an encouraging sign.

1 Secretaries of State for Health, Wales, Northern Ireland, and Scotland. *Medical audit. Working paper 6*. London: HMSO, 1989.
2 Royal College of Physicians. *Medical audit—a first report: what, why and how?* London: RCP, 1989.

Radical change of policy on NHS pay

Roger Dyson

The NHS review has two implications for pay: devolution and almost unlimited scope for self governing hospitals to fix their own terms and conditions of service. The latter will catalyse the end of national pay determination in the NHS, allowing such hospitals to recruit staff not only with enhanced pay but also better holidays and so on. One notable outcome of these proposals might be to attract staff by tailoring flexible packages of hours, holidays, and superannuation—but such a development would spell the death of the Whitley Council agreements.

The government's review of the NHS confirms a trend towards pay devolution already underway in Whitley council agreements and offers self governing hospitals almost unlimited scope to act independently in setting terms and conditions of employment.[1] These two developments constitute a remarkable change in policy and philosophy that will do more to change the character of the NHS than other more immediately visible changes in the review. In particular the rapid extension of pay devolution raises a longer term question about the future of the review bodies covering the pay of doctors, dentists, nurses, midwives, and other health professionals.

At national level the review makes clear that "the government's objective throughout the service is progressively to introduce greater flexibility in order to allow managers to relate pay rates to local labour markets and to reward individual performance." This process has already started and includes both grading and pay flexibility.

Two major grading flexibility agreements were introduced in 1988 for nurses and for medical laboratory scientific officers. Despite many faults, the clinical grading review in nursing has introduced a structure with several opportunities for grading flexibility and higher pay in the future. The introduction of more primary nursing and clinical nursing specialist posts is the principal opportunity for this flexibility. The scientific officers' grading flexibility agreement has been more radical. It offers the prospect of major changes in the mix of skills with the introduction of medical laboratory assistants and improved grading for scientific officers with more supervisory responsibility. By a judicious use of skills mix and grading agreements managers now have the opportunity to respond to local labour market difficulties by improving pay through the extension of job content within the framework of national grading agreements.

Staff side opposition

Now the Secretary of State envisages something more ambitious. Local pay flexibility has already been proposed to the nurses' pay review body in the management side's evidence, and in the current nego-

tiations with the administrative and clerical Whitley council the management's representatives are pressing for some local pay devolution on the back of a completely new and more flexible grading structure. In these negotiations the Department of Health gives the impression of being determined to press ahead irrespective of the opposition of the staff side to the principle of local pay devolution.

Much has yet to be decided about the range of pay flexibility, the degree of local discretion, and the extent to which regions will have to hold the ring to prevent a potentially harmful "bidding up" of the price of scarce professional skills. But the determination to devolve pay seems clear and has been forcefully confirmed in the white paper. Ministers seem to be determined to get the department out of the arena of pay determination over the next two years, and this creates greater doubt about the future of the Whitley councils.

One further important development occurred when general manager posts were taken out of Whitley pay negotiations for a separate settlement that included an important element of performance related pay determined at regional and district levels. Now this is being extended to a further 7000 posts at the next level of management with individual performance review and performance related pay. The growth of this trend in pay determination also undermines the Whitley pay bargaining structure.

This analysis of change in the national framework of pay determination is reinforced by the pay and conditions arrangements to be provided for self governing hospitals. Trustees are to be allowed to set their own pay and conditions for newly appointed staff; specifically they will be free "either to continue to follow national agreements or to adopt partly or wholly differing arrangements." There is, however, a constraint on the employment of junior doctors whose posts, states the white paper, "will continue to need the approval of the relevant royal college for training purposes."

> "... ministers seem determined to get the department out of the arena of pay determination over the next two years."

Trusts free to employ own consultants

Trusts are to be free to employ their own consultants on either a whole time or a part time basis and the NHS review seems to go out of its way to confirm that employment conditions need not be the same as those determined within the present pay review body. It almost goes without saying that managers in self governing hospitals will be paid on the performance related pay principle. "Performance related contracts

Department of Adult and Continuing Education, University of Keele, Keele, Staffordshire ST5 5BG
Roger Dyson, PHD, director

Br Med J 1989;298:654-5

of employment will similarly provide strong incentives for hospital managers to improve the quantity and quality of the services on offer."

It is the self governing hospitals and their freedom to determine pay and conditions that will act as the catalyst in bringing to an end the present national structure of pay determination in the NHS. A shortage among NHS professional staff already exists in the south east and is growing yearly. Several London teaching hospitals could not reopen clinical facilities even if money was provided because of the inability to recruit nurses and other key groups of scarce staff. Self governing hospitals would be free of restrictive Whitley conditions not just on pay but on the whole range of employment conditions such as the standard working week, the length of holidays, etc. That freedom would allow these hospitals to shape contracts that would be more attractive to scarce staff and so would start a migration of staff that would force the other major London hospitals to move quickly for self governing status in order to obtain similar freedoms.

For example, within the context of a hospital budget it would be inexpensive to make a major pay offer to the few intensive care and theatre sisters with the right qualifications needed to develop and expand major surgical services. This recruitment would be at the expense of neighbouring hospitals in London and would in turn prevent them from being able to offer a sufficient volume of NHS provision. The growth in waiting lists that this would entail would automatically push the "business" towards the self governing hospitals that had recruited the staff to take on the extra volume. Thus major hospitals that were not self governing would face either gradual decline or the prospect of following suit. Where staff is genuinely scarce and becoming scarcer competition for survival would be more ruthless. Where there were no major difficulties in obtaining staff the transition to the new régime would be far more gentle.

Response from general practitioners crucial

What could undermine this analysis would be the nature of the response from general practitioners and the public. If those patients needing cold surgery in the south east were prepared to travel to the midlands and the north and if general practitioners were prepared to send them because the costs were lower the strength of competitive pricing would put a curb on the ruthlessness of labour competition in London and the south east. If the geographical range of choice turns out to be much more limited this analysis of the impact of staff shortages is more relevant.

One further section on the future pay and conditions structure in the review offers more general hope. The government states its wish "to give local managers greater flexibility to determine the conditions of service of NHS staff . . . to enable them to devise employment packages that are most suited to local needs." In conditions of growing labour market scarcity the NHS as a public service can never hope to compete with the private sector on grounds of pay alone. The best hope for the future for any hospital wishing to make its staff less susceptible to higher pay elsewhere is to give them the opportunity to establish personal employment packages that are wholly flexible on matters of hours, holidays, superannuation, etc. Staff whose employers are prepared to tailor such packages are much more likely to stay and for longer. This is clearly going to be a developing service in authorities and self governing hospitals alike. But the offer of such personal packages to staff could be undertaken only if those staff were able to opt out of virtually all the terms and conditions of existing Whitley council agreements. This is as strong a reason as any for believing that the existing Whitley council framework cannot survive the introduction of the proposed changes.

Finally, in the famous teletext on 31 January a senior civil servant answered a question about the pay freedoms of self governing hospitals by referring to some vague wider framework within which they would operate. By contrast the Secretary of State continued to refer, in different ways, to the disciplines of competition. The battle over, the wider pay freedom of self governing hospitals may not yet be over.

Secretaries of State for Health, Wales, Northern Ireland, and Scotland. *Working for patients.* London: HMSO, 1989. (Cmnd 555.)

Theatre sisters: a seller's market

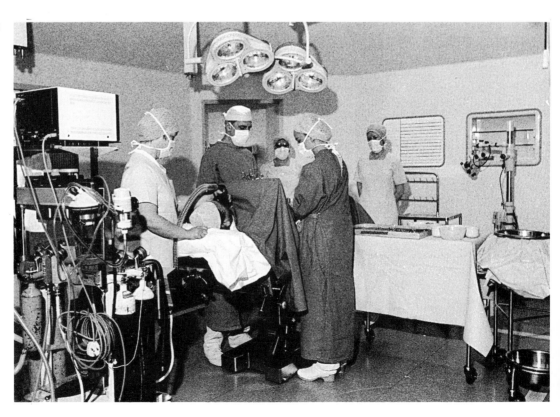

Aging—Should it be left to chance?

P H Millard, P Higgs, P Rochon

Proposals on the care of the elderly are conspicuous by their absence in the white paper, yet geriatrics represents a success story which Britain should support. Moreover, by 1996 the number of people aged over 85 will have risen from today's 603 000 to 894 000 – and they are likely to be more socially disadvantaged than younger patients. Market forces cannot underpin a policy for their care: what is needed is a professionally run service that puts patients first.

Department of Medicine, St George's Hospital Medical School, London SW17 0RE

P H Millard, FRCP, *Eleanor Peel professor of geriatric medicine*

P Higgs, PHD, *research fellow*

P Rochon, FRCPCAN, *honorary lecturer, supported by the Royal Canadian Legion*

Correspondence to: Professor Millard.

Br Med J 1989;**298**:1020-1

The government created the specialty of geriatric medicine within a national health service and the government is now destroying it. The specialty was created as a solution to misdiagnosis, mismanagement, absent teamwork, and lack of rehabilitation in local government run infirmaries. As a service of last resort geriatric medicine developed into a medical subspecialty concerned with the clinical, preventive, remedial, and social aspects of health and disease in elderly patients. It would be a disaster for the aged if our government, while introducing one American economist's dream, made the health care of the aged poor as bad as that provided in the country from which the fiscal dream emerged.[1] Certainly proposals on the care of the elderly are conspicuous by their absence from the white paper,[2] and by failing to respond to Sir Roy Griffiths's report on community care the government shows its indifference to integrated planning for acute and chronic care.[3]

In 1981 the government thought that it could no longer afford the specialty of geriatric medicine and turned to integration with general medicine instead. Some doctors argued that there was no organ system or procedure that justified the specialty's presence.[4] Sir Roy Griffiths considered that hospitals' responsibilities should cease at rehabilitation, and many managers, thinking of cost implications, support his view and are shedding responsibility for long stay care on to nursing homes.[3]

Those who want hospital consultants to shed any responsibility for long stay care fail to realise that responsibility not interest drives the wheel of rehabilitation. Consultants in geriatric medicine have clinical responsibility for the long term hospital care of patients in their catchment areas. They respond to this by developing strategies of care based on inpatient rehabilitation, day hospital provision, and coordinated aftercare. Theirs is a success story which our country should support.

Cooperation is basic to success

Illness presents differently in old age. Multiple pathology is the rule rather than the exception. Basic to success in caring for the elderly is cooperation with other specialties not the erection of defensive boundaries. In the United States the Institute of Medicine recognises the need for leadership by physicians in geriatric medicine because care of the elderly is complex and requires specialised knowledge.

Between 1986 and 1996 the number of people aged over 85 will grow by nearly a half; the over 85s have increased from 459 000 in 1976 to 603 000 today and will be 894 000 in 1996. This older group spends more days in hospital and uses a disproportionate amount of the health care budget.[5] Ignore their needs for specialist medical services and the whole house of cards collapses.

Plans to shorten patients' length of stay and to develop outpatient medical services may work for young people living with families but for the aged it is a non-starter. The over 85s are more likely to be single or widowed, to live alone, to be in substandard accommodation, and have income levels at or below the poverty line. To send such people home sicker and

> *"... basic to success is cooperation with other specialties not the erection of defensive boundaries."*

quicker causes them and the hospital staff extreme distress.[6] Such practices lead to rapid readmission and unnecessary permanent institutionalisation.

Political will is the problem

In the past 15 years there has been an unprecedented expansion in private rest and nursing homes.[7] Much of this expansion is funded by the patient and their families but part is funded by government. Government expenditure over the past decade on board and lodging allowances for aging people has increased from £7m in 1978 to £700m in 1987 and is still rising.[8] Clearly it is not money that is the problem; it is the political will.

A policy of relying on market forces within the private sector in the shape of rest and nursing homes will fail because the profit margin is dependent on beds being 100% occupied. Specialists in geriatric medicine choose to run their departments without waiting lists and work hard to keep some beds empty because they are trying to provide a rapid response service.

Economists state that demand for health care is infinite and resources are finite, but demand for long stay hospital care is not infinite.[9] There can be little doubt, however, that the number of people in care will expand to fill the resources available. Internationally the numbers of institutionalised people bear no relation to age, and nationally the expansion in private rest and residential homes is mainly at the seaside.[10]

51

Geriatric medicine should control that "attractor" by preadmission assessment, rehabilitation, and responsibility for medical aftercare. That was the original recommendation of the BMA in 1947 and it is now time for the recommendations to be implemented.[11]

Ever since the inception of the NHS responsibility for the medical care of the aged in institutions has been split between hospital doctors and general practitioners. In 1981, 42 health districts still had no geriatric beds on the district general hospital site. Rather than developing the hospital service the government chooses to spend the equivalent of 200 hospital beds a year on unsupervised, uncontrolled, unrationed care in private rest and nursing homes. This cannot be right.

Conclusion

The NHS, rehabilitation, and operational planning were the three health care legacies of the second world war.[12] Other countries are planning services based on specialist medicine and rehabilitation to cope with the demographic change: our government is content to let the invisible hand of market forces meet the needs of our aging population. This is too important a subject to be left to chance. The country needs a social policy run by professionals that truly puts the patients first not an economic policy to which entrepreneurs react.

1 Enthoven A. *Reflections on the management of the National Health Service.* London: Nuffield Provincial Hospitals Trust, 1985.
2 Secretaries of State for Health, Wales, Northern Ireland, and Scotland. *Working for patients.* London: HMSO, 1989. (Cmnd 555.)
3 Griffiths R. *Community care: agenda for action.* London: HMSO, 1988.
4 Leonard C. Can geriatrics survive? *Br Med J* 1979;i:1335-6.
5 Andrews K, Brocklehurst J. The implications of demographic changes on resource allocation. *J R Coll Physicians Lond* 1985;**19**:109-11.
6 Gerety M, Winograd C. Public financing of Medicare. *J Am Geriatr Soc* 1988;**36**:1061-6.
7 Phillips D, Vincent J. Petit bourgeois care: private residential care for the elderly. *Policy and Politics* 1986;**14**:189-208.
8 Day P, Klein R. Residential care for the elderly: a billion pound experiment in policy making. *Public Money* 1987:19-24.
9 Struthers J. The elderly in hospital. *Br Med J* 1963;i:470.
10 Grundy E, Arie T. Institutionalisation and the elderly: international comparisons. *Age Ageing* 1984;**13**:129-37.
11 Committee on the Care and Treatment of the Elderly and Infirm. Report. *Br Med J* 1947;i:133-40.
12 Timms O. Rehabilitation: to what? *J Am Geriatr Soc* 1967;**15**:709-16.

Geriatrics is a conspicuous British success—yet the white paper says nothing about the care of the elderly

The white paper and the independent sector

William Laing

Though under the white paper proposals private practice may expand considerably, there are real threats to it as well. A substantial fall in NHS waiting lists might diminish the attractiveness of private practice, and competition between NHS hospital trusts, other NHS hospitals, and independent hospitals might become more equal. Nevertheless, given the increased pressure to monitor consultants' fulfilment of their contracts, NHS managers may find it more difficult to cultivate consultants for help in private patient services.
Numerous collaborative ventures between the NHS and the private sector are in the pipeline at present and these new proposals will encourage them. One outcome might be to lower private fees for specialists, given their possibly reduced bargaining power if the basis of employment were to be altered to sessional work.

Working for Patients[1] has been enthusiastically received by independent sector interests. The NHS is to remain tax funded and this will be a disappointment to some diehards—though not an unexpected one. But any disappointment on this score is overshadowed by far by the prospect of private health care providers gaining access to what has hitherto been a largely closed NHS market. The white paper for the first time raises the real prospect of a single market for the delivery of publicly funded health care services, with public, charitable, and private suppliers competing on equal terms.

Exactly where the reforms will lead is hard to predict, since what is proposed is not so much a blueprint, like previous appointed day reforms, but rather a new framework for competition with all the uncertainty that entails. I can envisage greatly expanded private supply in some sectors. But equally there are real threats to the independent sector as currently constituted. I shall look at what the white paper might mean for the acute independent sector, firstly, in its traditional market—that is, privately paid or insurance funded services—and, secondly, in the new market that seems to be opening up, the NHS itself. In the absence of any white paper proposals on long stay and community care this important aspect of private sector activity is not covered.

Privately funded short stay health care

Medical insurance has been the engine of independent sector growth since 1948, accounting for 70% of the independent hospital revenue. The white paper proposes tax relief on medical insurance for people over 60. This is the measure that seems to carry least conviction among ministers at the Department of Health. Put in at the insistence of the Prime Minister, it has been dismissed in private as incidental to the main thrust of the NHS reforms. But what will its impact be? My own view is not very much. I base this on analysis of past trends. The figure shows that rates of medical insurance growth are only moderately responsive to price. People over 60 who pay tax, or family members buying insurance for them, will normally find their medical insurance premiums reduced by 25% and coverage can be expected to rise by somewhat less than 25%. Since people over 60 now make up a fairly small proportion of the medically insured population the new tax incentives are unlikely to make a substantial difference to the overall size of the medical insurance market. If, however, tax relief were to be extended to other age groups as well the impact would be that much greater. But as things stand those who dismiss tax relief for elderly people as a minor aspect of the white paper are probably right.

Tax relief will give an immediate if small fillip to medical insurance. But what will happen to the market in the longer term if the government's programme of NHS reform actually works? It would be wrong to characterise the growth of medical insurance cover as simply a manifestation of disillusionment with the NHS. Nevertheless, the most potent reason for taking out medical insurance is to avoid queues for NHS treatment. The state of the NHS waiting list at the time of the next election will be one of the key tests of success and there can be no doubt that the Department of Health will be trying its hardest to get this right. The NHS hospital trusts are going to play a crucial role here. They will have no incentive to keep large waiting lists, since money will move with the patient. Moreover, as the white paper says, maximum waiting times will be an important feature of contracts. It would be unrealistic to expect waiting lists to vanish, but if they were to come down sharply what effect would that have on public perceptions of the need to take out private cover? It is not impossible that medical insurers might see the attractiveness of their product undermined sufficiently to reverse the rising trend in medical insurance that has been with us since 1948.

Independent sector providers and the NHS

Despite the hype that has surrounded recent NHS contracts for private hospital surgery they still represent an insignificant part of the independent sector market. Taking acute medical and surgical

> "... once the traditional pattern has been breached ... competition could lead to a major restructuring of private practice."

treatment alone, independent hospitals earned only an estimated £18m out of their £542m revenue in 1987 from the NHS.[2]

London NW5 3ED
William Laing, BSC(ECON), *partner, Laing and Buisson*

Correspondence to:
1 Perren Street, London NW5 3ED.

Br Med J 1989;298:821-3

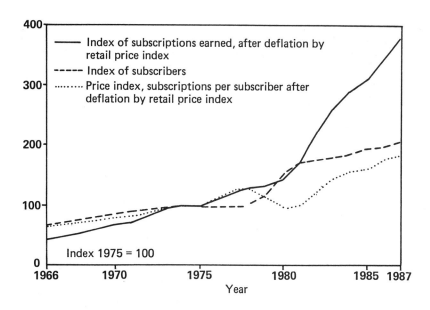

Medical insurance trends at constant prices after deflation by the retail price index, British United Provident Association, Private Patients Plan, and Western Provident Association data, 1966–87

population belongs to those practices of 11 000 or more which will have the option of running their own budgets, this proposal will not in itself lead to a substantial shift to supply by independent hospitals. Taken together, however, the reforms could in time turn the independent sector's present trickle of NHS short stay care contracts into—if not a deluge—at least a respectable stream.

Competition

The down side for independent health care operators is that health authorities and NHS hospital trusts will be encouraged to compete to provide services for paying customers. The process has already been set in motion with the Health and Medicine Act, which has given NHS units flexibility to develop and sell services at whatever prices they choose. There are already new NHS pay bed units—for example, in Bloomsbury and Hertfordshire—offering standards of amenity equal to private hospitals, and many more health authorities are attracted to their revenue generating potential. One of the big questions for independent health care operators, and here we are mainly talking about profit oriented organisations rather than the charitable and religious bodies that used to dominate independent health care, is how to face up to the challenge of dynamically managed NHS units.

The independents might pursue one of two strategies, or indeed both at the same time, to head off the threat.

● To engage in straightforward competition with the NHS for the limited number of private patients
● To get into bed with the National Health Service.

As to the first strategy, such competition as has taken place to date has gone almost entirely the way of independent hospitals. In 1982 the overall revenue of NHS pay beds was about level pegging with independent hospitals. But by 1987 it had dropped to about one eighth of independent sector earnings. The

In the post-review NHS health authorities will be free to buy services from private hospitals. That in itself marks no change. What will be different is that the whole system will gradually be geared to buying and selling services. Here again the NHS hospital trusts will play a crucial role as catalyst. The fact that health authorities will routinely be buying services from NHS hospital trusts will give them the skills and the information to seek possibly more attractive terms from other suppliers, including private hospitals. Moreover, the proposal for capital charging, whereby health authorities will pay for the cost of the assets they use, will put competition between NHS hospital trusts, other NHS hospitals, and independent hospitals on a more equal footing. As well as health authorities, general practitioner budget holders will be able to contract directly with independent hospitals on behalf of their patients, though since only 9% of the

How will independent units—such as the new paybed unit at Walsgrave Hospital, Coventry—stand the competition from dynamically managed NHS units?

question now is whether the new type of NHS pay bed unit, run as a business rather than an underused convenience for local consultants, can halt and reverse this decline. NHS pay bed units will have many advantages, including convenience for consultants. But my guess is that the conflict inherent in running public and private services in parallel will weigh heavily against them. NHS managers and health authority members will remain vulnerable to the charge that private services are receiving resources to the detriment of public services.

NHS managers will also be placed in a difficult position with consultant staff. The white paper proposes fuller job descriptions for consultants than is commonly the case at present to enable district management to monitor whether consultants are fulfilling their contractual obligations. As providers of public services, NHS managers will be under increasing pressure to monitor consultants' activity more rigorously and not to be slow in pointing out deficiencies. But as providers of private patient services, dependent on consultants to bring in business, they will have to develop entirely different relationships. Health authorities may find it difficult to cultivate consultants as effectively as independent hospitals, and this may be a critical factor limiting their ability to compete effectively against independent hospitals, assuming consultants remain the principal source of private referral (see below).

Collaboration

The other strategy open to independent sector interests is to get into bed with the NHS by convincing health authorities or NHS hospital trusts that their objectives can best be met not by direct competition but by joint ventures of one sort or another, including privately financed or managed pay bed units. In time this might lead to the emergence of a new type of NHS and private management company as a major force in private acute health care and even the transformation of the independent sector as we know it.

There has been a surge of interest in joint ventures and partnership proposals in the past two years relating to a whole range of health care services aside from pay beds. Some collaborative arrangements for ordinary district services have already been set up. These include a novel scheme in Coventry, where Bioplan Holdings plc has provided the capital for a new private patient ward, a day surgery unit, and an endoscopy unit at Walsgrave Hospital, to be managed by the health authority, which will in turn sell capacity back to Bioplan for private patients' use. There is hardly a major independent health care group that does not have a dozen or more collaborative ventures at some stage of the pipeline from discussions in principle to heads of agreement. The white paper states the government's determination to encourage these schemes where they are consistent with value for money and proper control of public expenditure, and clearly the NHS environment will become more supportive as the white paper proposals begin to take effect. The proposed freedom for NHS hospital trusts to borrow from the private sector will create new opportunities for joint ventures while capital charging will further encourage health authorities fully to utilise their land assets. Spare NHS land is frequently the basis for mutually beneficial collaborative schemes.

Restructuring private specialist services

There is another way in which the white paper's proposals might bring a restructuring of private health care. So far, when talking of the independent sector, this has referred to hospitals and clinics only, which earned an estimated £542m in 1987. But an additional £302m went on surgeons', anaesthetists', and physicians' fees. Whereas private hospital costs are usually comparable with, and often lower than, NHS hospitals, private medical and surgical fees are much higher than equivalent medical and surgical labour costs in the NHS. In part this reflects the bargaining power of the medical profession in their dealings with private insurers and in part it represents a tacit understanding that the NHS can offer fairly low pay rates on the understanding that many of those hospital doctors who become consultants will then be able to benefit from the much higher unit pay for private practice. No one has yet seriously challenged the private fee structure for specialists though there is an increasing awareness that substantial savings could be made for private patients if, say, hospitals were to employ their own specialists to undertake operations on a sessional basis. This would involve a major change in the traditional route of patient referral, which is through consultants who then choose the hospital. And it would clearly meet with strong resistance from privately practising consultants.

The establishment of NHS hospital trusts could well be the catalyst that destabilises the present structure. These trusts will be free to set pay and terms for their consultants—and other staff—as they wish. The first ones to be set up are also likely to include some of the most prestigious hospitals in the country. It is not hard to imagine the sort of arrangement that might emerge, possibly in association with an innovative insurance company seeking a preferred provider relationship, whereby the hospital itself would become the key focus of the referral chain and the full time consultants working for the NHS hospital trust would be compensated sufficiently to exchange that for the traditional pattern of private practice. Once the traditional pattern has been breached it is then not hard to see how the forces of competition could lead to a major restructuring of private practice in Britain.

1 Secretaries of State for Health, Wales, Northern Ireland, and Scotland. *Working for patients*. London: HMSO, 1989. (Cmnd 555.)
2 Laing W. *Laing's review of private healthcare 1988/89*. London: Laing and Buisson, 1988.

Words from the source—an interview with Alain Enthoven

Richard Smith

Much of the thinking behind the government's review of the NHS originated with Professor Alain Enthoven, who is professor of public and private management at the Graduate School of Business, Stanford University, and one of America's leading experts on the economics of health care. In 1985 the Nuffield Provincial Hospitals Trust published a book he wrote on the NHS after visiting Britain and examining the service closely.[1] His main proposal was for an experimental internal market. We sent him copies of the NHS review and the working papers, and Richard Smith spoke to him in California.

"I cannot understand why the government did not choose to test these very promising ideas in a series of pilot projects."

RS: What was your initial reaction on reading the white paper and the accompanying working papers?

AE: Generally very positive. I see several good ideas, but I also find it hard to understand just how the government's proposals would work in practice. I felt the need for diagrams and more explanation of how they would work. The details can be very important.

RS: And you didn't find that you got that in the working papers?

AE: No I was very surprised by the lack of detail. I would have expected definite and specific information on how this would work in practice.

RS: One of your reactions must have been that this is your own ideas being taken up?

AE: Yes, although I would have been pleased to see them worked out in more detail. I thought that I was throwing out a general idea that needed to be developed.

RS: Some people have suggested that it isn't for the government to provide detailed proposals. Rather it should set a direction and people in the health service could then work out the details for themselves. Do you agree?

AE: The government is asking a non-accountable industry to become accountable. It is attempting to introduce some competition into a non-competitive service. I think that it is asking too much for the government to expect the health service to do it itself without a good deal of direction from the government. Many important questions will have to be asked and answered in detail before such a scheme can be put into practice. For example, who decides, and on what criteria, whether a hospital can become a self governing trust? What happens if such a hospital and a health authority that depends on it cannot agree on prices? Perhaps the people in the health service can work out the details for themselves. But I would expect some of the questions to raise fundamental policy issues that the government will have to decide.

RS: And you think that must come from the government?

AE: Yes.

Strong and weak points

RS: What did you think were the strong points of the proposals?

AE: At the broadest level I thought that the NHS needs to separate the demand and the supply side: by that I mean that institutions independent of the production of the services have to be setting standards and priorities, measuring achievement, and seeking value for money. In my 1985 report I recommended that the district health authorities be recast as purchasers of services on behalf of the populations they serve, with choice of where and from whom they buy the services, rather than being cast as monopoly suppliers of

"I see several good ideas, but I also find it hard to grasp the overall concept."

services to the people in their districts. It is allowed to set its own standards and measure its own achievement. How does anybody know whether it is performing as well as it should? Until now the NHS has been a monopoly—as if we at Stanford said to students, "You can set your own exams and grade them."

I see several important steps towards separating the demand and supply sides in the government's review. One is self governing hospitals. Another is the idea of a mixed economy with private hospitals able to compete for NHS patients, as they do to a limited extent today. Another idea is that regions would all receive their main budget allocations on the basis of population, adjusted for age, morbidity, and the like with adjustments for cross boundary flows replaced by direct payments among regions. Thus their budgets would be based on estimated need not on the services they produce.

Another very strong idea is that money follows patients. Today a hospital that does a great job of producing high quality care efficiently is likely to get more patients without correspondingly more money—not a very good incentive.

Greater delegation to the local level is a good idea.

Some experimentation with budget holding by general practitioners is an idea well worth exploring, though I have reservations about how the government proposes to do it.

Involving consultants in management responsibility is an important idea. Increasing the authority of district general managers over the appointment and rewarding of consultants in order to reward those who contribute most to maintaining and improving local services is an excellent idea.

The proposed scheme to charge districts for using capital assets—therefore rewarding those that use capital most efficiently—represents a major step in the direction of economic efficiency. The proposals to strengthen medical audit are also important and valuable.

If I were British I would certainly applaud "appointment systems which give people individual appointment times that they can rely on" and "clear and sensitive explanations of what is happening."

In short the review sets forth many good ideas that definitely ought to be part of a reformed NHS.

RS: So you see lots of strong points. What about weak points?

AE: The main weak point must be the lack of specificity about how the good ideas will be put together in a working system.

". . . tax relief for private health insurance . . . that has been a disaster for us in the United States."

RS: Were there no specific points that made you think "My goodness!"

AE: The only thing like that was the proposal of tax relief for private health insurance. My reaction to that is "watch out." That has been a disaster for us in the United States.

RS: Why?

AE: Because it costs the federal budget a great deal of money—about $40 billion a year—and works to encourage the choice of a more costly rather than a less costly health scheme. And most of the money goes to people with high incomes, who don't need an incentive to buy enough health insurance, rather than to people on lower incomes who do.

Self governing hospitals and general practitioner budgets

RS: Two central proposals in the review are that hospitals should become self governing and that large general practices should hold budgets. How do you react to these?

". . . society has legitimate concerns about the quality, economy, and efficiency of care, and if you don't like the way that the government is going about it then you should come up with better ideas."

AE: It is part of the separation of the demand and supply ideas. In my 1984 visit I saw Guy's Hospital, a magnificent institution, being ground down by application of the RAWP (resource allocation working party) formula because there wasn't enough demand for services in its own district. Meanwhile, patients in other districts not far away could have been well served by Guy's. My feeling is "let Guy's compete to serve them." As a self governing NHS trust it will be free to do so.

Letting hospitals negotiate their own pay scales will be a step forward. One district general manager told me that one of his main problems was keeping surgeons supplied with good secretaries. It can be a terrible waste of time for a surgeon to have to spend lots of time correcting and editing notes because he or she doesn't have a good secretary. But the district included the headquarters of a great corporation that kept hiring the best secretaries for more money. The manager said he would have to obtain the personal approval of a minister in London to match the pay of the private sector. The process would doubtless have been matched by arguments about fairness: why should she be paid more just because the private sector is offering her more money? The NHS pays a big price for overcentralisation.

I'm concerned, however, by the possibility of monopoly pricing—by which I mean that a hospital may feel that it can get away with charging much more than it may need to if it's the only hospital within a convenient distance.

RS: How could that problem be overcome?

AE: One option would be to pay hospitals prospectively by diagnosis related groups as one medicare programme does. That option should be looked at.

RS: What about budgets to general practitioners?

AE: It is an interesting idea, but I have reservations about the government's proposals. Firstly, a practice with 11 000 patients is too small to support the management expertise that is needed to do a good job of purchasing hospital services. General practitioners haven't been trained for that complex task. It would have been better to coalesce five or six such practices—

to reach over 50 000 patients. I think, too, that it will be necessary to develop capitation fees that relate to the health risks of the patients. And 11 000 is too small for risk spreading.

General practitioner budgets would have been a good subject for a pilot project.

Objections from general practitioners

RS: General practitioners in Britain are one of the groups most unhappy with the government's proposals. They worry that they will be pressurised to take on more patients, that they may have to work within cash limits, and that patients will be shunted around the country, making continuity of care very difficult. Do you sympathise with these worries?

AE: This makes me think of the worries of American doctors. I say to them that society has legitimate concerns about the quality, economy, and efficiency of care, and if you don't like the way that the government is going about it then you should come up with better ideas.

RS: That's a general response. What about the specific worries I've mentioned?

AE: I trust general practitioners to take sensible decisions and not take on more patients than they can handle. But there should be rewards for those who work harder and satisfy their patients. The problem of exceeding budgets is a complex management issue. I would presume that health authorities would not stop payment but rather encourage overspending general practitioners to look at their practices and find ways to reduce cost.

RS: What about the problem of patients being shunted around from one end of the country to another?

AE: I think it's too easy to exaggerate the extent of being shunted around the country. For most people it would not mean going very far, and if it means having your operation done promptly by very skilled people then it may be a small price to pay to have to travel. People already travel for specialised services.

A two tier system?

RS: Some people in Britain are worried that these proposals might lead to a two tier system. Do you think that may happen?

AE: I think that Britain already has a system with various tiers in terms of quality of care and service, though they are not measured and documented. The reforms will not make it worse. Indeed, they might make it better. The main two tiers at the moment are the public and private services, and under the new proposals poorer people will have access to private hospitals. If the government's objectives are met service in the lower tier will improve.

RS: Another worry is that the proposals may be the prelude to full privatisation. Do you think that's likely?

AE: I don't think so at all. That is using extreme rhetoric to try and cloud some important issues of how to get more efficiency, innovation, and quality out of the system.

Information

RS: Let's talk about the problem of information. Much information that is not currently available will be needed to operate the new service. Do you think that generating the information will present serious problems of timing and expense?

AE: Management information is important, and the NHS must get on with producing it. My impression in 1985 was that there was a remarkable lack of information in the NHS. For instance, the NHS does not know the cost per case of a coronary artery bypass in one hospital compared with another or the risk adjusted mortality in one hospital versus another. Such information is important because there are wide variations in costing and mortality. One hospital may cost two or three times as much as another. Similarly mortality rates may vary widely. Here in California, for instance, risk adjusted mortality from open heart surgery varies from 1% in the best hospitals to almost 18% in the worst.

RS: But such figures are hard to interpret.

AE: They are, but it's important to get on with it. Do the research that's needed to improve the systems. Quantified measures of outcome are definitely the way to go.

RS: But isn't this expensive. Will the information pay its way?

AE: If I thought I was going to need a bypass graft operation in California information on risk adjusted mortality at different hospitals would be worth a lot to me.

One cannot prove that systematic collection and analysis of data on quality and cost is worth the money. But I notice that every successful company in a competitive service or manufacturing business finds it worthwhile. There isn't one that doesn't do it. Why should the health service be different?

Florence Nightingale called for such information over 100 years ago. Modern information technology is making it practical to collect it.

Pilot studies, timing, and outcome

RS: You made great play in your book of the importance of pilot studies, but the government has decided against such studies. How do you react to that?

AE: I think it's a mistake. Demonstration projects are a very good idea. Proposed innovations should be developed locally with people who are keen to try them. The bugs can be ironed out, and then others can be brought in and shown how well the system worked and encouraged to participate. I cannot understand why the government did not choose to test these very promising ideas in a series of pilot projects. Health care is an institution that is very difficult to change. There is much uncertainty, and so much is at stake. So people are reluctant to change. That reluctance may be broken down by successful pilot projects.

RS: The government plans to have this system up and running by 1991. Does that seem to you a realistic timetable?

AE: Considering the large changes that will have to be made—in information systems and culture—that's an amazing speed. Health care just doesn't change that fast.

RS: Finally, the government said in its white paper that it had two main aims—to give patients better health care and greater choice of services, and to achieve greater satisfaction for those working in the NHS who successfully respond to local needs and preferences. Do you think that it will achieve those aims?

AE: A more decentralised flexible model with more consumer choice and accountability could lead to these goals. Somewhere in the government's territory offered by the proposals there is room to achieve those goals, but I don't understand fully how the scheme is going to work and I think progress will take time, development of systems and expertise, and cultural change in the health service. Don't look for some big improvement overnight.

1 Enthoven A. *Reflections on management of the National Health Service.* London: Nuffield Provincial Hospitals Trust, 1985.

Letters to the *BMJ*

The *BMJ*'s readers – those who see the patients and will have to make any new organisation work—have also been thinking through the implications of *Working for Patients*. Here are the letters on the NHS review that the *BMJ* published from 18 February to 15 April.

General principles

SIR,—We welcome the resident population funding approach which is used in the white paper *Working for Patients*. The previous approach (Resource Allocation Working Party) has been reasonably successful in moving towards equity between regions but has not achieved equity between districts.[1] This continues to be shown by the wide variation in hospitalisation rates per 1000 standardised population (DHSS performance indicator A1, which ranged from 74 to 148 in the 191 English districts in 1986-7, with an average of 108 for England).

We hope that resident populations will be defined using general practice lists as the basic building blocks. This will require each family practitioner committee to hold lists for whole general practices rather than the current system using geographical boundaries, and should enable each family practitioner committee to become coterminous with its main constituent health authorities.

This approach will have a number of advantages. It should simplify organisational relationships and financial responsibilities between general practitioners, family practitioner committees, and health authorities; strengthen the role of general practitioners as the gatekeepers to the NHS as a whole; ensure that all services, including preventive programmes such as immunisation and breast screening, can be more easily planned, delivered, and evaluated; and help the health authorities to discharge their responsibilities for the health of a defined population according to the requirements of circular HC(88)64.[2]

In implementing the proposals in the white paper we must not allow the excitement about self governing hospitals to distract us from the population based approach to health care which is fundamental to the NHS. We are pleased that the Secretary of State has confirmed his commitment to this approach as outlined in HC(88)64, and we regard primary care and the definition of health authority populations as being crucial to success.

To ensure that the new health service works for populations as well as for individual patients a director of public health must be an executive member of every new health authority, alongside the general manager and the finance director. Otherwise, directors of public health and health authorities will be unable to fulfil all the requirements of HC(88)64 and the white paper.

ROGER SIMPSON
ELIZABETH HAWORTH
NICKY WHITAKER
PETER DIXON

Department of Public Health Medicine,
West Berkshire Health Authority,
Reading RG3 4EJ

1 Simpson RJ, McCloskey BG. Sub-regional revenue allocations and SMRs: progress towards equity? *Hospital and Health Services Review* 1987;83:165-7.
2 Department of Health. *Health of the population: responsibilities for health authorities.* London: DHSS, 1988. (HC(88)64.)

SIR,—The white paper appears to suffer from two major omissions and one potential major contradiction.

Firstly, there appears to be no intention to improve the information system. At present there is no way in which the NHS at any level can obtain reliable data about the prevalence of disease in any local population group. Even data on incidence are not sufficiently detailed or reliable because the current methods of coding and the level of staff who do it leave something to be desired. It is therefore difficult for planners to assess the required level of provision of health services.

Secondly, there is very little reference to preventive medicine and public health generally. It is axiomatic that reduced disease prevalence would reduce the requirement for curative health services —for example, tuberculosis in the United Kingdom—and we still have major problems with, for example, ischaemic heart and other vascular disease and lung neoplasms.

Finally, charges for capital assets are to be introduced. These will presumably form a significant cost element in the financial calculations which are to be a prominent feature of the yet again reformed NHS. There are several ways in which such charges could be calculated.[1-3] Account will have to be taken of inflation, local differences in property costs, and equipment depreciation. If calculated on true local values the charges for property in urban areas, especially central London, will make all procedures rather more expensive in the major urban hospitals, considerably to their detriment under the present plans.

It may be that these problems will be addressed in the detailed further papers to be produced. If they are not I would suggest that we are not going to see any real advance in the effectiveness of the NHS following these new plans.

P M BRETLAND

London N6

1 Owler LWJ, Brown JL. *Wheldon's cost accounting.* 15th ed. London: Pitman, 1983:chapter 13.
2 Bretland PM. Costing imaging procedures. *Br J Radiol* 1988;61: 54-61.
3 Bretland PM. Costs of nuclear medicine. *Nuclear Medicine Communications* 1988;9:37-42.

SIR,—The government's white papers on the future of the NHS, *Promoting Better Health* and *Working for Patients*, sound good.

The first contains a series of fairly minor changes to the NHS which are largely irrelevant to health. Ill health is still mostly caused by poverty, unemployment, bad housing, polluted environments, poor education, smoking, drinking, unsuitable food, accidents, and social isolation. If the government cares about health it could accept the World Health Organisation's recommendations and adopt coherent policies to tackle these things.

The second could perhaps be better named *Working for Profits*. The changes it suggests, though major, are still mainly irrelevant to health. What they will eventually achieve is a much more expensive system with widely differing standards according to the patient's wealth.

If this is what we want—Amen. If not, we should say so loudly now. All who care should write to their members of parliament before the proposals are discussed in parliament.

E T SCRASE
N JONES
S M LESLIE

Llanidloes,
Powys SY18 6EZ

SIR,—I read Dr Gordon Macpherson's editorial[1] with rising irritation. Perhaps it suffered unduly by following on the intelligent and open minded review by Ms Patricia Day and Professor Rudolf Klein.[2] I am myself a sceptic who does not believe that the promised land is often entered by the gate of reorganisation, but the manner and matter were peculiarly provoking.

The editorial started badly by saying that the association's leaders are "doubtful that the promise in the white paper's title, *Working for Patients*, will materialise." This was followed by a statement that it would be unwise to make a policy response until the working papers had been analysed and finally that the council and craft committees should have time to consider the proposals. But the policy statement was already implicit in the first sentence quoted; in the simplest terms, "We don't like it and don't think it will work." The generally hostile tone seemed to imply a further statement—"We don't like Mr Clarke," perhaps? Or "We don't like the government"?

The second paragraph seemed to be in danger of

coming to grips with reality. The BMA's response is indeed risky in the face of a secretary of state in a hurry. And why does Dr Macpherson believe that neither of the two radical proposals "can be achieved without the cooperation of most NHS doctors." As he himself says, "Kenneth Clarke is a formidable minister who is backed by a Prime Minister with a large parliamentary majority." The NHS will be reorganised and it will be generally on the lines of this review. None of us may like it but carping articles like this can only make matters worse.

He also regrets that the BMA's excellent advice—that any new ideas should be tried out in pilot schemes—are out of time. This is not a moment to be looking over our shoulders at what might have been. The BMA represents most, but not all, of the doctors, who in turn are a small minority of the NHS staff; they are not the government, they have had their say, and they did not persuade. If they cannot come to terms with this they will achieve nothing but harm for their members. A sullen resentment of the government plan as a whole is the worst possible response. The review is published and the political facts are that everyone is stuck with it. The constructive response is to cooperate fully and even enthusiastically; in that way it should be possible to strengthen all that is good and reduce or even eliminate what is dangerous. Politics, like medicine, is the art of the possible. The political situation, like the patient, is a fact; it may be unfortunate that the patient has scabies and it may be unfortunate that the NHS has Kenneth Clarke, but in both cases that is the starting situation so let's be positive and see what we can do about it. In neither case is it useful or prudent to give way to distaste or regret; that can only inhibit effective action.

We have seen this minister in action before on issues like the limited list. Offended dignity and the moral high ground have not proved effective in the past, nor will they now.

J K DEWHURST

Finchampstead,
Near Wokingham,
Berkshire

1 Macpherson G. BMA's measured response. *Br Med J* 1989;298:340-1. (11 February.)
2 Day P, Klein R. NHS review: the broad picture. *Br Med J* 1989;298:339-40. (11 February.)

SIR,—There has been much recent talk of improving the efficiency of the National Health Service, with attention being directed particularly at the role of administrators and doctors.

The users of the health service, the public, also have a major contribution to make in this respect, as highlighted by a recent audit of attendances at the Lothian area colposcopy clinic in Edinburgh, one of the largest in the United Kingdom. Between 1 August 1988 and 10 February 1989, 7769 appointments were made for the clinic, and 2552 (33%) of these were not kept. In 1259 instances the patients did not even notify the clinic of their inability to attend; some did not attend on several occasions.

We appreciate the anxieties of our patients and therefore go to great lengths to inform patients of the nature of their conditions and the procedures entailed in investigation and treatment so that some of their understandable worry may be quelled. Every patient is sent an explanatory leaflet before the first visit, and afterwards the necessity for follow up visits is explained. The patient is given a mutually convenient appointment before leaving the clinic.

Non-attenders take up the time and energy of already overworked staff and delay appointments for other patients, some of whom will have invasive cancer. Is it not time for the public to realise that they too have some responsibility for improving the efficiency and quality of the National Health Service?

WILLIAM HELM
GEORGE E SMART
JEREMY R B LIVINGSTONE

Royal Infirmary of Edinburgh,
Edinburgh EH3 9TW

SIR,—White papers in the health service are like movie blockbusters in reverse. *Jaws 1* was riveting and a box office hit but *Jaws 2* had limited appeal. White paper 1 (1987) *Promoting Better Health* attracted some attention but white paper 2 (1989) *Working for Patients* is going to run and run.

Now that the razzmatazz of the announcement of the NHS review has died down, attention is focused on the working documents that were expected to provide the "nitty gritty" of how the brave new world of the NHS will function but are notable in their lack of detail.

The need for greater accountability is incontestable. Closer scrutiny of both hospital and general practice services must be a laudable aim. Acceptance of a ceiling on health care costs cannot be avoided. It is the notion of health care being bought and sold as a market commodity that raises fundamental questions about the possible lack of safety nets within a restructured health service.

Having worked at the sharp end of primary care in North America and had first hand experience as a patient in the United States, I have found that there is little true appreciation in the United Kingdom of how market place medicine leads to adversarial relations among hospitals, among practices, and above all between doctors and patients.

Parallels can be drawn with what has happened in universities, where money is in danger of becoming the only applause for a good performance. The frequent end result is that institutes of higher education become top heavy with low priority being given to groups who, through no fault of their own, are unable to generate substantial amounts of income.

Though the government will claim that hospitals and practices have a choice in opting for the holding of budgets, there seems little doubt that the long term aim is a shift of attitudes about the provision of medical care. If nothing else the white paper serves an important function in allowing people to think through how best to move forward. When considering the specific proposals for market led initiatives it would seem prudent to inch forward by degrees, while insisting on a rigorous appraisal of untested ideas and constantly asking, in terms of health care, whether something that is profitable is always worth while.

JOHN BAIN

Aldermoor Health Centre,
Southampton SO1 6ST

SIR,—In Dr Stephen Lock's trenchant editorial on the new government proposals he refers to the fear that they could lead to a two tier structure both in hospitals and in general practice.[1]

Surely we already have a two tier hospital service with the NHS in the professional lead. The NHS provides a comprehensive crisis medical service, which deals with most of the serious sudden medical and surgical illnesses and does it most competently. There is still some room for improvement, but both for individual patients and for major incidents the service is efficient, comprehensive, and nation wide backed by teams led by consultants. The private sector has neither the beds nor the resident staff to deal with such emergency work. It has the edge on the NHS for elective work and with its greater amenities (but is serving as a pathfinder for the NHS). The greatest single benefit of the NHS has been to provide a remarkably even distribution of consultant skills around the country, and I doubt if this will be affected adversely by the government's proposals.

In my retirement it is inappropriate for me to comment on the details of the proposals. May I make one general remark, however, having worked as a consultant both before the NHS and for many years with it? Each year the number of inpatients treated has steadily increased and has reached about 6·5 million, 3·5 million more than in 1948. Paradoxically, each year the number of beds used has fallen and is now at least 150 000 fewer than in 1948. These changes can be represented graphically as two straight lines, one up and one down. Neither of the previous reorganisations have made an appreciable impact on these graphs (except for a small hiccup in 1974), nor, I think, will the present proposals. The process of eliminating unnecessary

Mrs Thatcher on Panorama: the start of the media management

duplication of services, thanks to medical progress, will continue as before.

I shall remain an optimist, trusting in reason, man's natural intelligence, and his conscience. The silent majority in this country have long realised that after the old age pension the NHS is the next best innovation this century.

F AVERY JONES

Pulborough,
West Sussex RH20 2HE

1 Lock S. Steaming through the NHS. Br Med J 1989;298:619-20. (11 March.)

SIR,—Ms Patricia Day and Professor Rudolf Klein state that Alain Enthoven advocated budgets for general practitioners (for hospital care) as part of the internal market.[1] This is the opposite of the case. Enthoven saw general practitioner budgets as damaging to rational decision making by district managers; it is the managers who would trade with each other (hence the internal market). Enthoven made this clear when I worked with him at the Nuffield Trust in 1984 and 1985 and has recently reiterated the point forcefully in a letter to me. I think it is important to point this out, given the political momentum behind general practitioner budgets in the wake of the white paper.

CALUM PATON

Centre for Health Planning and Management,
University of Keele,
Keele ST5 5BG

1 Day P, Klein R. NHS review: the broad picture. Br Med J 1989;298:339-40. (11 February.)

SIR,—We are led to believe that £1m has been devoted to informing us of the hotchpotch of ideas that have been put together as a white paper to reform the National Health Service. It is clear that the authors of the paper took pains to remain uninformed about matters of health care, and the result is that they have prepared a disastrous plan that is being "sold" very effectively.[1]

It is tempting to take the pragmatic view that the present government is so impregnable and so determined to put its vision into practice that the best course is to accept the inevitable and try to obtain the best interpretation of the broad themes that have been promulgated in the interests of our patients, practice, hospital, or whatever.

This is likely to prove a dangerous and damaging course in the longer term, for if a firm and accurate assessment (and rejection) of these ill conceived initiatives is not provided by the profession they are in effect given credence by acceptance.

We have a responsibility to redress the balance. May I suggest that the BMA in conjunction with other responsible professional bodies, perhaps aided by sponsorship, seeks to provide an educational programme to inform the public of the wrong headedness of the government's new approach and spend a similar amount on this vital project to that which has been devoted to spreading the alternative gospel.

DAVID JOLLEY

Withington Hospital,
Manchester M20 8LR

1 Black D. Kind of health care we do not want. Guardian 1989 Feb 6:20 (col 2).

✲✲The secretary writes: "Our primary concern has been to ensure that the profession is fully informed on the government's proposals. A BMA video highlighting the key proposals has been sent to every division, a special newspaper was produced, and slides have been made for speakers to use at meetings of doctors. The public and MPs have been informed of our initial views through a major media campaign and extensive parliamentary lobbying. A special briefing conference for interested organisations is being planned. Additional channels of communication with the public, MPs, and other organisations will be used as the profession's views are formulated."—ED, BMJ.

SIR,—We note the comment in Dr Stephen Lock's editorial that the Conference of Medical Royal Colleges and Faculties in the UK has not responded separately to the white paper on the NHS.[1] The Joint Consultants Committee agreed that a unified response from its two constituent bodies—the conference and the Central Committee for Hospital Medical Services—would properly reflect the opinions of all hospital doctors. The views of the conference have been incorporated in the submission of the Joint Consultants Committee to the social services committee of the House of Commons. In due course the conference may need to respond to specific points in greater detail.

SIR IAN TODD

Conference of Medical Royal Colleges and their
Faculties in the UK,
Royal College of Surgeons of England,
London WC2A 3PN

1 Lock S. Steaming through the NHS. Br Med J 1989;298:619-20. (11 March.)

SIR,—Only a wild romantic picks a fight that he or she cannot hope to win, and the BMA seems to be doing just this in its response to the white paper.

If we take a firmly antagonistic line to all the proposals we shall be seen as hopelessly reactionary, conservative, and perhaps even avaricious as well as lazy. This government is strong enough and willing to enforce its way not only on us but even on the legal profession.

If we continue our rigidly negative stance we shall have no influence on developments. Unless we are more positive towards the inevitable we cannot possibly influence developments more to our liking. Vast amounts of money will need to be invested in information technology; not just in computers and programs but also in the enormous amount of work entailed in extracting data from notes, many of which are badly kept. The cost of information technology for hospitals and practices has been estimated at about £1 billion, and this might not include the many hours of processing the data. If we have to meet the cost from our own budgets and recoup it from expenses in subsequent years it will mean a substantial fall in profits.

Another important aspect that needs influencing is the proposed payments for immunisations and cervical smears only if targets are reached. Practitioners who fall well short of the targets may give up even trying while the goalposts are being built on wheels so that targets can easily be made unrealistic. We need adequate safeguards.

The white paper is not all bad; it represents an important step in the direction of relating pay to work. Many of the changes outlined are already applied by some of the more innovative practices, but the investment in equipment and staff and their time means that such practices are out of pocket for their efforts. The public, the electorate, our patients, or whatever you like to call them, will judge us harshly if we stand like King Canute in the way of change. Let us face reality and make the most of it. Express deep reservations by all means, and if the change is a failure then we can say, "We told you so!" If it is a success we can claim the credit. Thus we win both ways, but with blind opposition we lose both ways.

PAUL HEWISH

Goole,
North Humberside DN14 6AW

SIR,—As one who has worked in industrial medicine for many years I was particularly interested to see the request from a nearby hospital for industrial sponsorship—requests that are likely to increase if the recommendations in the white paper on the NHS come into force.

At first reflection I could see little reason why industry, which already produces the taxes to support fully the National Health Service, should provide further funds through sponsorship. But perhaps the answer would be an improved hospital service, specifically for industry. Thus, the following might apply: (a) industrial evening clinics and special shift worker clinics; (b) weekend appointment systems for outpatients; (c) priority industrial surgical waiting lists for hernias, slipped discs, and the like; (d) weekend and evening arrangements for physiotherapy and rehabilitation; (e) free health checks for shift workers at weekends; (f) priority facilities for immunisation for overseas sales personnel; (g) improved communications with industry about sick employees and hospital care; (h) secondment of medical students to study industrial problems during training and in immediate postgraduate training.

Such services as these might well attract interest in sponsorship from industry, which would certainly be looking for evidence of interest in its problems, and might well help with many of the problems that concern large industries today.

G C MATHERS

Taynton,
Gloucestershire

SIR,—May I suggest that Dr Stephen Lock's belief that the government is steaming through the NHS is incorrect? I believe that its tactics in the NHS review follow the classical pattern of attacking on several fronts when the aim is to secure only a single objective. Thus of the 16 proposals I have identified in the review, I believe that only one has to be secured for the government to achieve the change that it regards as essential in the functioning of the NHS.

To provide the additional care, identified by all professionals with an interest in the NHS, at no additional cost the government has chosen to extend competitive tendering to the clinical services provided by hospitals.

My experience on the General Whitley Council and in my own hospital is that the competitive tendering process results in low priced tenders being accepted, with an appreciable saving in expenditure at a cost of reduced quality of cleaning and ancillary services.

I believe that the extensions of competitive tendering to the clinical care of patients will have this result unless the medical and nursing professions stand firm about the quality of care provided to patients. All the other proposals within the review that affect medical staff have the primary purpose of intimidating consultants so that management can force them to enter into clinical competitive tendering at reduced cost for the care of their patients.

The application of budgets to general practice will assist the government in ensuring that patients are sent to the hospitals that have been prepared to reduce their cost of patient care in line with its thinking. If general practitioners refuse to support the competitive tendering process it will fail.

Hospitals opting out of the NHS will create a climate in which competitive tendering will become far more intense as the independent boards managing them will have far less medical representation than existing district health authorities and have the power to "hire and fire." Managers of such hospitals will be able to force compliance on their medical staff.

A great Victorian, John Ruskin, once said: "There is nothing which cannot be made more cheaply and less well." The British public deserves a health service which has been properly made and adequately funded.

J M CUNDY

Lewisham Hospital,
London SE13 6LH

1 Lock S. Steaming through the NHS. *Br Med J* 1989;298:619-20. (11 March.)

SIR,—The Department of Health has set up a helpline for general practitioners to telephone with queries about the new contract to be imposed next year. With dogged persistence I managed to speak to the medical officers three times, but they were unable to be any more specific about the contract. They seemed surprised that the document shows a reduction of income for the present workload, described in the examples as "kept to the minimum," and that it would take considerable extra work to maintain income, never mind increase it to levels which are only theoretically possible (and out of which expenses have to be taken). They were full of blandishments, yet our livelihood is at stake.

The numbers concerned meant that the medical officers would each have to speak to about 200 general practitioners a day for five days a week over the three weeks of the helpline. Despite being overwhelmed they still went home at 5 pm. General practitioners are to provide times for consultation convenient to patients yet the department was not prepared to set the good example of providing an adequate service at times convenient for general practitioners.

After three weeks the helpline ceased, leaving a recorded message giving an address to send comments to. The message lasts 25 seconds, the address only six seconds, and it is not repeated. I would be found in breach of my terms of service for such a brief, indistinct message for my emergency telephone number. The department's poor example rankles.

C D E MORRIS

Walsall,
West Midlands WS5 3AD

Effects on general practice

SIR,—In their editorial on the NHS review Ms Patricia Day and Professor Rudolf Klein point to a "conspicuous and entirely lamentable failure to give the government's response to the Griffiths report on community care despite the obvious implications for the role of the district health authorities."[1] I endorse that criticism. I have just spent a day at my surgery in central London. At lunchtime the practice partners met with the district nurses and other members of the primary health care team, who are supposed to look after people in their own homes—I had visited four elderly people, three women and one man, and the complaint was always the same—"the community services are just not available." The visits of home helps are minimal, and the visits of nurses to help elderly people with bathing are so infrequent and irregular that some elderly people refuse them when the nurses do call and because of the restrictions they do not call again. The district nurses are each covering the work of two, can only just manage with their workload, and cannot take on a new patient unless another is removed. Only the meals on wheels service gets a universal hooray, although the quality is variable, according to those who take it regularly.

Discussing the problems with the practice team, I found almost universal gloom about the ability of the community services to cope at present, let alone when the hospitals send patients home even earlier to maximise their "throughput and turnover." One of the four patients I had seen clearly could not be adequately looked after at home and had to be admitted to hospital; the others will remain in the community only if the resources are there to maintain them in a warm, humane, and decent environment.

The health authority is unable to achieve its quota of district nurses and is desperately short of health visitors and community psychiatric nurses. The social services do not answer the telephone let alone take a referral of a patient in distress. When they do take a referral a visit may have to wait for a few days because of the pressure of emergency work. The inevitable consequence is that we tend to carry on regardless because we cannot turn away patients' requests for help, and we are forced to admit more people, especially the elderly, to hospital.

Our patients and the team also complain about the ambulance service. Nearly 30% of our elderly patients who have outpatient appointments are not collected because of shortages in the ambulance service, and patients complain also of waiting for hours to return home. One diabetic woman needing regular food intake had to wait until nearly 7 pm before she could be taken home. Another patient, who is partially sighted and unable to walk far, missed three outpatient appointments for her eyes. When the ambulance had not come on the fourth occasion I felt that I had to take her myself.

The review of the NHS, *Working for Patients*, is irrelevant to most of the needs of elderly patients.[2] What they require is a caring, compassionate, friendly, and available service, not one that is rushed off its feet, short of staff and facilities, and always facing yet more cutbacks and restrictions.

The drive for cost effectiveness and efficiency should start with caring for people in their own homes and communities, not in buildings and organisations. Unless we get that straight what use is there in screening, early diagnosis, and treatment? Care is what we are there to provide.

JOHN COHEN

London W1P 1HL

1 Day P, Klein R. NHS review: the broad picture. *Br Med J* 1989;298:339-40. (11 February.)
2 Secretaries of State for Health, Wales, Northern Ireland, and Scotland. *Working for patients.* London: HMSO, 1989. (Cmnd 555.)

SIR,—Many of the "changes" advertised by Kenneth Clarke at a cost of over £1m took place months or years ago in South Humberside without the noise accompanying the launch of the white paper.

Drive around local villages and towns and you will find bright, well appointed buildings where patients are seen on Saturday mornings and bank holidays as well as during the week. Even where most of the work is carried out "by appointment" patients who feel that their problem will not wait for the first available appointment can be seen without an appointment within 24 hours (often well within five hours) on weekdays.

At night and at weekends and even at Christmas and Easter all of the calls are dealt with by local general practitioner principals, and when necessary the doctors are happy to visit. That is not all. As well as all the basic surgery equipment there are often electrocardiographic machines (costing over £1000), autoclaves (also £1000), blood glucose monitoring machines, and sigmoidoscopes in the surgeries. These cost money to run and provide no increased income. Though they are a definite financial liability they are also a financial demonstration that the doctors care for the health of their patients.

Several local practitioners have been performing minor surgery regularly for many years. One practice's recent records showed over a score of procedures carried out, ranging from one patient whose accessory nipple was excised through 43 operated on for epidermal cysts to 106 on whom vasectomy had been performed. Individual doctors have their own special interests, and as a result there are many practices with well woman clinics, well baby and child assessment clinics, antenatal clinics, special investigation and surgery sessions, with some practices offering psychotherapy, hypnotherapy, acupuncture, and homoeopathy.

Practice nurses have played an increasing part, and one nurse has set up a walk in health check and screening clinic for her practice's patients. Such a service can be provided only with the support of other professionals such as community sisters and practice nurses, and some of the work they do generates extra income, but part of the salaries of practice nurses comes from doctors' own pockets.

The government talks about support in the future for computerisation. Many of our practices have systems "up and running," and others are planning to introduce them. With well organised practices the computer gives a massive improvement in patient care and saves the Department of Health money—for example, from more efficient prescribing—but it provides doctors little in the way of extra earnings.

The profession's aim has been an average list size of 1700 patients—to allow time for doctors to look after their patients properly—rewarded with proper remuneration. The government is now proposing that a much greater proportion of doctors' remuneration should be based on the number of patients on their lists. Already one local practice that was about to take on an extra partner —not to attract more patients but to permit the development of a more comprehensive service with more screening and special illness group clinics—is having second thoughts.

Will it be last decade's medicine next decade?

T J GRATTAGE

Scunthorpe,
South Humberside DN16 2RS

SIR,—The National Health Service is under threat from a government which does not understand the relationships between doctor and doctor and doctor and patient, on which the effective practice of medicine depends.

General practitioners under the leadership of the BMA can help to safeguard the NHS if they will do three things: (1) refuse to agree to any promotional advertising; (2) refuse to enter into financial arrangements with any NHS hospital for treating NHS patients; (3) refuse to accept any limitation on present referral arrangements.

There are many other important issues, which the BMA will no doubt take up with the government, but these seem to me to be critical.

JOHN PEMBERTON

Sheffield S30 1AG

SIR,—The government's new contract for general practice has much to commend in it.[1] The government has reaffirmed the leading role of general practitioners in primary health care.

We will not have to increase our list size. If we run a full range of services we can maintain our income with a smaller list, providing more care to fewer patients.

The new commitments will make a strong practice team essential. Practice nurses will be far more effective at health education than doctors. Doctors who invest in good staff, good premises, and good relations with the health authority will be able to meet realistic targets for health promotion.

The General Medical Services Committee must ensure that targets are realistic, and 80% for cervical cytology screening would be a strong incentive for us to give up our screening programme. More importantly the committee must ensure that the government will fund, and continue to fund, the staff and premises necessary to run a preventive service. This is a new and additional service. Initially it may be funded by redistribution among general practitioners, but ultimately new money must be forthcoming as more practices meet their targets.

The new contract is, on the whole, good for patients and good for doctors. We should support it and negotiate the small print.

A MORGAN
P BOWER
SALLY BARNARD
CHARLOTTE BIRD

London SW12 8EA

1 Department of Health and Welsh Office. *General practice in the National Health Service: a new contract.* London: DoH, 1989.

SIR,—Mr Kenneth Clarke has suggested that individual general practitioners should express their views on the new government contract for general practice. I think it is vital that we do so now.

The stated aim of the new proposals is that they should make general practice more responsive to the needs of the consumer. I hope we can assume that this means the patient. Studies of what patients want from their general practitioners consistently find that they want a doctor who listens, who understands, who takes trouble, and who explains. In other words they want an unhurried, competent, personal doctor whom they can trust when they are sick. Anything that militates against that most basic and legitimate need is against their true interest.

Our existing contract has some serious defects in this respect but the one now proposed seems to be a great deal worse. By encouraging competition linked with cost containment it must increase the pressure for shorter and "cruder" consultations. By introducing arbitrary financial incentives for such activities as well person clinics, whose value in the form proposed is unproved, it will further erode the doctor's time for traditional consultations. The central dominance given to cost control will introduce a new factor in the doctor-patient relationship for which both patients and their general practitioners are unprepared. I fear that it will endanger the quality of that relationship.

Patients commonly take for granted that their doctor is competent. The need to ensure that that trust is justified should be the most important element in any good contract for general practice. The proposed new contract will seek to do this by forms of external control. This cannot be effective except in preventing the crudest level of incompetence. The effective way to improve quality of care in general practice is by performance review conducted by a practice on its own work, leading to agreed decisions and actions. Such activity needs to become an integral element in the working lives of general practitioners. If this is to become a reality it must in some way have "protected time." Instead of recognising this the new contract will make this type of professional learning compete for practice time with other activities which will carry persuasive financial rewards. I fear that formative self assessment based on shared review of clinical work will be the loser—together with the patients of course.

The need for selective rewards for good work and for quality control are not in question. They are both essential to encourage good general practice. The current proposals, however, achieve neither of these things. They come to us as an arbitrary package of crude bribes to undertake activities whose value, in some cases, has never been properly tested. They have been presented with an arrogant and, in my view, mistaken belief that their originators know what is best for patients and for general practice.

In their present form the proposed new contract is unacceptable.

IAN TAIT

Aldeburgh, Suffolk IP15 5HG

MONITOR SYNDICATION

The composition of the cabinet committee to review the NHS was never made public, but, as well as Mrs Thatcher, it consisted of Kenneth Clarke (Secretary of State for Health), David Mellor (Minister for Health), John Major (Chief Secretary to the Treasury), Malcolm Rifkind (Secretary of State for Scotland), and Peter Walker (Secretary of State for Wales)

SIR,—When I was young many doctors seemed to drive expensive cars. I and some others tried to economise by driving small cars. These reduced expenses were reported in our tax returns, and the government reflected them in reducing that part of our gross income that related to our cars.

A similar (and perhaps more serious) mechanism applied to the expenses of our surgeries: today's economies became the standard by which future allowances were based. I believe that the government is offering us another treadmill that looks very attractive but shares this problem. We can have budgets. If we economise we can spend the savings on our surgeries. But what evidence have we got that if we make economies the size of our budgets will not then be reduced?

The result of these treadmills for the profession is not progress from our running but angina.

JOHN TROWELL

Harlow, Essex

SIR,—At its meeting on 10 March an overwhelming majority of the council of the Royal College of General Practitioners opposed the principles of the white paper and declared its solidarity with the General Medical Services Committee of the BMA.

According to my notes of the meeting, of 18 members of council who spoke, only four fully endorsed the keystone of the government proposals—the shift to internal and external markets in the NHS. As these were Drs Marshall Marinker, John Fry, Donald Irvine, and vice chairman Dr Colin Waine, however, their arguments need more than gut unity to refute them; and despite his vigorous, unifying, and courageous reply to Kenneth Clarke's aggressive speech at the council dinner the night before Professor Dennis Pereira Gray's discussion paper for council rested on an interpretation of history which will ultimately lead to capitulation if accepted.

Though the entire package has been cobbled together by people who fear their Prime Minister more than they respect evidence and is therefore full of practical inconsistencies, if we are to be understood by the public we must defy its unacceptable principles rather than doubt its unworkable mechanisms. That defiance must rest on understanding rather than instinct, which means that the whole membership of the college should join the debate with this authoritative, experienced, and well informed minority of our leaders, whose beliefs have led them to agree with the fundamental principles of the white paper despite the overwhelming opposition of their colleagues.

Themes developed by Drs Marinker, Fry, Irvine, and Waine were, respectively, the necessity of leadership, lifting the profession above the immediate reactions of most to higher planes of statesmanship; the incorrigible conservatism of general practitioners, who resisted Lloyd George in 1912, Nye Bevan in 1948, and Margaret Thatcher in 1989; the necessity of competition if we are ever to deal with the bad practice we all know exists; and a plea for understanding that the minister must know what he's doing and should be given a chance. Admitting a fondness for history, Professor Pereira Gray gave us his interpretation of it: how a health service designed for the poor is bound to change now that we are rich. As he pointed out, a substantial minority are not rich. They must be provided for, and this really worries him. He is genuinely torn between the demands of realism and sentimentality: no prizes for guessing the outcome of any conflict seen in these terms.

These five views are quite simply wrong; not marginally but utterly. In any society advancing toward rather than retreating from civilisation greater wealth should mean better public services. When we were poor we knew how to share, but the world's task is to learn how to share riches not poverty. The chancellor has just declared the biggest ever budget surplus; if we accept an underfunded NHS in such circumstances we betray everyone who slaved to create the opportunities we now enjoy. Kenneth Clarke's evident intelligence is no guarantee that he can know the consequences of plans that have never been piloted; unit costs even for such commonplace procedures as cholecystectomy simply do not exist.

We have bad doctors and bad hospitals; all

doctors and all hospitals are bad some of the time, and a few are bad all of the time. What is the opposite of competition? Cooperation: and that is what we were just beginning to see as we painfully emerged from the dark ages of dog eat dog and unscrupulous patient pinching. I have seen my local district hospital develop, through bitter struggle in which there were enemies as well as friends, from a third rate hospital going nowhere to a second rate hospital with increasing self respect. Competition is fine for winners, but what about losers? In any foreseeable competition my local hospital and the people in it will resume their roles before the NHS as losers unless they can afford to go to Swansea or Cardiff. Our reactionary profession is deplored but, led by our college, there has been a sea change in general practice since the 1966 Charter. Overwhelmingly, general practitioners now accept that they provide a public not a private service. This must entail public accountability to an elected administration and responsibility to patients as health producers. What we are being offered are the risks of an adversarial market with entrepreneurial doctors who must learn to advertise and consuming patients who will learn to use lawyers. Kenneth Clarke's reference to general practitioners who reach for their wallets when they hear the word "change" is not only insulting but stupid; if he has not even noticed that we are now ready to discuss clinical audit in practical terms this shows how uninterested he really is in the few positive and progressive proposals contained in his document.

Finally, Dr Marinker speaks out for leadership. Leaders should stand for the recivilisation rather than decivilisation of our critically sick society. The government cannot understand that the cash free economy of the NHS, which has given us not only a more humane but also a more economic service than any of the international models with which it has been compared, is a more advanced social form than the efficient but profit oriented industries of commodity production. But we understand it and so should our leaders.

Our college can and must join with others to repeat the success of the 1966 Charter in the more difficult, dangerous, but at last more hopeful circumstances of 1989. With its call for a properly funded NHS without major managerial reorganisation, the House of Commons Standing Committee on Social Services has a better heart and brain than any we have seen in the Cabinet and genuinely represents the balance of constituency opinion. If we practise open and democratic medical politics we shall have a united profession backed by most of the people, who never gave nor were asked to give any mandate for the white paper or anything remotely like it. The divisions will be on the other side, and they will soon appear.

JULIAN TUDOR HART

West Glamorgan SA13 3BL

SIR,—Many members of the Royal College of General Practitioners have been disturbed to note the premature and at times wildly exagerated response of some of the college's leading lights to the NHS review paper. Even if the government's plans for general practice were going to be twice as successful as some of our luminaries believe it would have been wiser for them to have contained some of their enthusiasm until the membership had had a chance to voice its opinion.

Of course, no one denies that the leadership of any institution has a role in shaping the attitudes and expectations of its members. But, surely, ultimately it must be the members who should have the final say. After the "Belton affair" and the "North East Thames fiasco" there was a faint hope that some lessons might have been learnt. But, alas, that does not seem to be the case. Shooting oneself in the foot seems to have become the habit

of a lifetime. To many general practitioners, maintaining the current momentum for change in general practice, which has already achieved outstanding successes in terms of patient care, would have been ideal, especially bearing in mind that this has all been achieved by a sensible process of education and persuasion.

JAMIE BAHRAMI

Postgraduate Dean's Office,
University of Leeds,
Leeds LS2 9JT

SIR,—Dr Julian Tudor Hart's letter has done great disservice to the profession's reaction to the NHS review.[1] The government has gained strength from divisions between the BMA and the Royal College of General Practitioners; Dr Tudor Hart, by quoting colleagues, has furthered division within the college.

Political convictions developed in Glencorrwg are not applicable generally. We hope also that readers will not be taken in by emotional language and meaningless phrases such as a society "retreating from civilisation." The trouble with the health service has been its patchy performance and wasteful use of resources. Rejecting the white paper outright simply gives credence to the sinister statement recently made by the Secretary of State for Education, Mr Baker, when he said to his opposite number in Portugal recently: "All professions are a conspiracy against the laity."

The proposal for practices to produce an annual report must be welcomed as much more information is required by consumers. Who other than the lazy can object to the practice of audit? One of us (MKT) has been largely responsible for proposals to conduct regular assessment of the over 75s, rather than simply being paid 37p a month extra for an older age group, which is neither an incentive nor a reward. This is progress in an aging society. On the other hand, there are aspects that are retrogressive, such as reintroducing competition and head hunting, larger lists, limited partnerships, and bleak employment prospects for young doctors and women doctors.

Dr Tudor Hart's verbose letter (greatly exceeding your 400 word limit, by 135%) showed an unimpressive lack of discrimination but, instead, incrimination of other council members and the president. The minister is willing to listen to intelligent, reasoned comment at the grass roots and is already prepared to make concessions as a reasonable man. Compared with systems on the continent many aspects of general and hospital practice need improving—for example, reluctance to do home visits, long waiting lists, and a lack of scanning technology. The probability is that we spend more time discussing, while doing less, than more practical nations. But the statement that "the entire package has been cobbled together by people who fear their Prime Minister more than they respect evidence" is a hollow jibe from one who has elsewhere pointed to grave deficiencies in primary care education.

There has rarely been a time when political will to improve the delivery of health care has been so clearly defined. The need now is for professional guidance rather than prejudiced rebuttal.

M KEITH THOMPSON

Croydon CR0 5NS

BASHIR QURESHI

Hounslow West,
Middlesex TW4 7RS

1 Hart TJ. RCGP's reaction. Br Med J 1989;298:888. (1 April.)

SIR,—The debate about the government's white paper Working for Patients and the new contract for general practitioners seems to generate much heat but little light.

The main arguments of those challenging the proposals of these documents are that giving general practitioners budgets, making them aware of the economic effects of their decisions, and encouraging them to work efficiently will lead to a poorer standard of service for patients and that the new contract will change the doctor-patient relationship. I have not seen any evidence for these assertions.

Any doctor as a servant of the community has a responsibility to use its resources prudently. If doctors are asked to do the sums they can produce evidence to satisfy themselves that they are fulfilling this duty. There is no evidence that prescribing and referring patients to hospital prudently leads to any worse standard of care or worsening of the doctor-patient relationship. In my practice our prescribing costs are 20% below the average for the family practitioner committee, and in a recent survey we referred patients to hospital in only 4·8% of our consultations. I have never had patients complain that I was penny pinching in my prescribing or that I was not referring them to hospital when they should be seen there. One reason why we refer so few patients to hospital is that we practise planned, structured follow up for our patients with asthma, diabetes, hypertension, premenstrual tension, and menopausal symptoms. We also have child development clinics, screening clinics for adults and the elderly, antenatal clinics, and two minor surgery lists each week. Our patients do not suffer from being followed up in the practice rather than in hospital. We have carried out audits of our follow up of chronic diseases,[1][2] counselling services,[3][4] hormone replacement services,[5] services for opiate addicts[6] and the elderly,[7] screening,[8] consultation arrangements,[9] and referral to hospital.[10]

In what way would our patients suffer from our using some of the money saved from a budget by not prescribing unnecessary antibiotics for sore throats or not referring patients for follow up at hospital diabetic clinics to buy a spirometer for our asthma clinic? Our patients know that at the moment we spend money for such items out of our own pockets. I do not believe that they would think any less of us if we bought such items out of money saved from a budget.

In conclusion, we are not a special practice staffed by academics. We do not exclude difficult patients from our lists—we look after 40 opiate addicts. There is no reason why any practice should not do what we are doing—and do it more efficiently on a budget.

EDWIN MARTIN

Bedford

1 Martin E. Audit of diabetic care. J R Coll Gen Pract 1988;38: 123-4.
2 Martin E. Monitoring the care of hypertensives. Physician 1986;5:677-80.
3 Martin E, Mitchell H. A counsellor in general practice—a one year survey. J R Coll Gen Pract 1983;33:366-7.
4 Martin E, Martin PML. Changes in psychological diagnosis and prescription in a practice employing a counsellor. Fam Pract 1985;2:241-3.
5 Colebrook M. Hormone implants. Update (in press).
6 Martin E. Managing drug addiction in general practice, the reality behind the guidelines. J R Soc Med 1987;80:305-7.
7 Harrison S, Martin E, Rous S, Wilson S. Assessing the needs of the elderly using unsolicited visits by health visitors. J R Soc Med 1985;78:557-61.
8 Shepherd P, Martin E, Carson I. Health screening by a nurse in general practice. Br Med J 1985;290:1792.
9 Martin E. Consulting patterns. Comparison between doctors' perceptions and patient behaviour. J R Coll Gen Pract 1987;37:23-4.
10 Martin E. Referral to hospital. Update 1987;34:556-60.

SIR,—Fired by the notion of achieving an immunisation target but rather quizzical about the ability of the system to reflect accurately work that is being done, I examined the authority's computer printout relating to my last clinic.

There were nine unscheduled attenders. Twenty appointments had been sent out; six children attended and were fit for immunisation and 14 did not attend. Of the non-attenders, eight had already been immunised but the computer had failed to record this; one was a known refusal; and one had moved from the list. Six therefore had "failed to attend."

The lessons to be learnt are that a 90% target is no easy bullseye and that each practice will have to keep immaculate records of work done. We need to look closely at the comparative response rate between authority recall and practice recall. We have been running an immunisation clinic in our surgery for 10 years with active cooperation of health visitors. I would not be confident that we could achieve the 90% target on the minister's terms.

P M J O'DONNELL

Luton,
Bedfordshire LU3 3AH

SIR,—Having read the white paper and working papers relating to *Working for Patients* and *General Practice in the NHS—a New Contract*, I am appalled and saddened.

Having graduated as a mature student in 1975 and spent four years in hospital medicine satisfying the criteria for vocational training, I entered the general practitioner trainee year, leaving behind—with considerable relief—what I felt to be the impersonal conveyor belt system of hospital medicine and hoping that I would at last have time to be a caring doctor and friend to my patients.

I was fortunate to be asked to join my trainee practice, now a partnership of seven, as a principal—fortunate especially as the emphasis was on a fairly small list size, now between 13 000 and 14 000 patients, permitting more time and better care for the patients, although, admittedly, lower remuneration. At that time (1979-80) the aim within the NHS was to reduce still further individual general practitioner lists, the optimum number of patients proposed being 1700.

As I understand the recommendations of both white papers, *Promoting Better Health* and *Working for Patients*, the new emphasis is on competing for patients to accrue as large a list as possible (*a*) to prove what good doctors we are (though it is commonly recommendations from existing patients that determine list size, not the range of services available) and (*b*) to try to maintain our salaries at a reasonable level after the government has withdrawn more than 50% of the current fees and allowances.

How can this possibly benefit individual patients who already think that the proportion of the doctor's time they rceive is totally inadequate?

General practice is currently far from perfect, but this is, in part, already due to pressures resulting from trying to be all things to all people to too many patients. I agree that more time needs to be spent in health education, but I submit that this has a far greater impact on the patient if it is offered in the context of the current consultation than as a sterile exercise in a special clinic. Many general practitioners already do child health surveillance whereas others prefer, as do many patients, that this is practised in local authority clinics. Bonus payments encouraging all general practitioners to undertake this duty are surely the prelude to abolishing the clinics. Would one minor operating session of five patients a month really represent a huge saving in hospital resources?

The primary requirement of every patient is that his or her general practitioner is readily available for consultation when the need arises, whether it is physical, mental, or psychosocial, and current proposals will reduce that availability by encouraging hours spent in running superfluous clinics, preparing reports and statistics, and ensuring that all our energies are directed into exercises which offer specific remuneration. Are we going to allow the government's latest exercise in ill informed interference to destroy the paramount needs of our patients, or are we going to offer a united front to oppose what is, in effect, yet another cost cutting exercise?

SUE McFARLANE

Surrey GU18 5SQ

SIR,—It is only right that patients should be able to make an informed choice of doctor, and reasonable that doctors who provide extra services should be rewarded, as should those who take advantage of postgraduate education. It is arguable that this should be at the expense of other doctors.

What is of grave concern to all doctors is the government's proposals for family practitioner committees. The local medical committee is to be rendered redundant, and local representation is to be removed from the family practitioner committee. A small group of people appointed directly by Whitehall will therefore hold power over the profession; that power is potentially far reaching, including (1) influence over the appointment of replacement partners; (2) power to inspect not only premises but also staff, logistic systems, and practice policies; (3) power to take sanctions over prescribing; (4) power to monitor not only referral rates but also the reasons for referral; and (5) power of veto over the general practitioner's place of residence.

There seems to be no obligation on the family practitioner committee to act on or even take medical advice, which can be commissioned from various sources and therefore is in no way independent. In addition, there is no mention of right of appeal.

The government obviously intends to emasculate the profession as a prelude to complete removal of independent contractor status, and as in previous conflicts it will use the tactic of divide and rule. In this case the potential wedge is between the Royal College of General Practitioners and the BMA, but both organisations have much to fear from the erosion of professional status.

We must unite to fight for the power of self regulation, and resignation would not be too strong a measure. If we concede to regulation by lay administrators then we simply cease to exist as a profession.

L J BURNS
M J RAMSDEN
G H J HANCOCKS
H P WATSON

Wakefield WF1 4PR

SIR,—Many of your correspondents, like Dr Paul Hewish,[1] have an unfortunate tendency to confuse the government's proposals in the white paper *Working for Patients* with those in *General practice in the National Health Service: A New Contract.* This is presumably why you publish letters on both subjects under the general heading "NHS review."

Although there is some overlap between the two sets of proposals, they have very different implications. It is therefore essential that we respond to them separately. It is perfectly logical—and probably politically more effective—to oppose one but not the other.

The white paper is about fundamental changes to the NHS as a whole. It has no clear commitment to more money for NHS services—the only commitment on financing the NHS is that it will continue to be "financed *mainly* out of general taxation" (my italics). Although its stated objectives, such as more audit, are welcome, the core of its proposals relate to the imposition of an untested market oriented system on the NHS. Anyone who believes that such proposals are misconceived and likely to damage the interests of patients has every reason—a duty, even—to oppose the white paper. There is nothing blind about such opposition.

Most of the contract proposals are about the way general practitioners are paid and will affect patients much less directly. Some of them certainly need to be withdrawn or modified, including the unrealistic nationwide targets for immunisation and cervical screening and the obligation to carry out health promotion activities for which there is no clear evidence of effectiveness. However, let us demonstrate how reasonable we are by negotiating on the contract while opposing the white paper.

JOHN TEMPLE

Nottingham NG7 1QG

1 Hewish P. NHS review: no hope in blind opposition. *Br Med J* 1989;298:889-90. (1 April.)

SIR,—Like Dr A Morgan and others[1] we are general practitioners in London who are enthusiasts for health promotion. We regard their enthusiasm for the new contract for general practitioners, however, as both naive and ill thought out.

The central drive of the contract—that is, a sharp increase in the element deriving from capitation—is thoroughly retrograde. It will force list size up and consultation time down. Single-handed colleagues will be driven to extensive non-NHS work to maintain their income, and incoming vacancies will become still rarer. The target figures for vaccination and cervical cytology are simply unobtainable in inner cities given the problems of list inflation, patient turnover, and ethnic minorities. Indeed, it seems to us quite extraordinary that anyone with a knowledge of modern urban practice would ever draft such proposals. The contract itself is wedded to the white paper's philosophy of competitive marketplace care, which is an inappropriate and inefficient method of health care provision. Inner city doctors like ourselves are likely to be especially penalised by the white paper's plans as hospitals opting out will probably leap frog over us and our patients to do business with megapractices holding budgets in the affluent south east. The community health services, which we find so valuable in health promotion, would be marginalised by the white paper's proposals.

The contract for general practitioners needs to be developed, and a few of the features in the proposed draft, such as an allowance for social deprivation, are appropriate.[2] But the philosophies of the present draft, its effect on general practitioners' income and terms of service, and the arrogant manner in which it is being imposed are unacceptable.

DAVID WIDGERY
FELICITY CHALLONER
ANNA LIVINGSTONE

London E14 8HQ

1 Morgan A, Bower P, Barnard S, Bird C. NHS review. *Br Med J* 1989;298:747. (18 March.)
2 Widgery DJ. *The national health.* London: Hogarth, 1988:78-81.

Effects on hospital practice

SIR,—With the government's proposals under discussion for the NHS our experiences are relevant.

In the past few years we have watched with dismay the gradual and inexorable decline in the facilities we offer acutely ill patients in London. There are fewer medical beds, the rate of turnover is higher, nurses are more stretched, there are fewer of them, and there is no continuity. Equipment is often old and not renewed, and there is no direct access to modern investigations such as computed tomography, nuclear magnetic resonance, or even coronary angiography, but a high medical standard is still expected. We are told constantly about the increasing investment in the NHS, but it has certainly not been our experience.

We see money spent on absurd grandiose projects —for example, our new geriatric block is to be knocked down a year or so after it was opened; it is well built, full of fine, airy rooms and lavishly furnished. When the new psychiatric block was planned it was to be on the site of a splendid Victorian hospital chapel. The workmen were just completing the new chancel roof while the demolition men were at the other end knocking it down. Yet the basic facilities for acutely ill patients are often appalling and get no better.

Our fear is that by default the true situation is unknown to the general population. In the newspapers we read uninformed criticism of doctors that they exaggerate, and "shroud waving" is one of the terms used when we comment about dangers as we see them; politicians are no better nor more responsible. Most of us hold our peace as we have never registered every catastrophe or near miss in our medical practice. As a result we prepared a prospective study of our acute general medical admissions on a one in four rota to a busy central London district general hospital, recording the patients to whom we were not able to offer the appropriate medical care and whose lives were needlessly put in peril. Over the three months of the study we have collected 12 case records of patients from a total of 102 patients.

Case 1—A woman aged 42, who was a chronic alcoholic, severely dehydrated, and hypotensive with a secondary supraventricular tachycardia. No intensive care facility was available; she was transferred to a coronary care unit 5 km away during the night.

Case 2—A man aged 28 who had taken a large overdose of hyoscine butylbromide required ventilation. No facilities were available. He was transferred 5 km at midnight with our anaesthetist giving manual ventilation. He survived.

Case 3—A man aged 70 with acute left ventricular failure one week after myocardial infarction, who did not respond to treatment and required ventilation. No intensive care bed was available; after two hours spent telephoning 13 hospitals he was eventually transferred 16 km at 2 am. He required two weeks' ventilation and survived.

Case 4—A woman aged 75 in a hyperosmolar, non-ketotic coma with acute renal failure for whom no intensive care facilities were available. She subsequently died despite biochemical measurements showing no abnormalities.

Case 5—A man aged 60 with acute myocardial infarction for whom no facilities for close observation were available. He was placed in a geriatric ward and survived.

Case 6—A woman aged 22 with severe, acute asthma, who waited for two hours in a surgical ward for an intensive care bed for ventilation while her condition deteriorated. She survived.

Case 7—A woman aged 47 with neurogenic pulmonary oedema secondary to subarachnoid haemorrhage. She was intubated, ventilated, and transferred 5 km for intensive care facilities. She died.

Case 8—A man aged 46 with staphylococcal meningitis with a caudate nucleus abscess and an anterior spinal artery thrombosis causing a T10 paraplegia who had an 8 km journey for adequate neuroradiological facilities and waited nine months for orthopaedic rehabilitation. He survived but was paraplegic.

Case 9—A woman aged 68 with acute chronic left ventricular failure who was sent home as no hospital bed of any sort was available. She was admitted some days later and survived.

Case 10—A woman aged 26 with a first episode of acute asthma for whom a private surgical side ward was the only accommodation. She was never monitored because a peak flow meter was not available. She survived after a stormy convalescence.

Case 11—A woman aged 76 admitted for dental clearance who waited one week in a surgical ward without her normal diuretics, resulting in acute left ventricular failure. She died awaiting her operation.

Case 12—A woman aged 51 who deteriorated postoperatively after a gastropexy and had clinical features of pulmonary embolism on two separate occasions. No facilities for pulmonary angiography were available; streptokinase was given blind. She died; at necropsy her lungs were congested but no embolus was apparent.

It is a sad reflection that such things should happen. The period we describe is typical, and we are confident that it represents the usual state of affairs in any other three months during the past five years; we know our colleagues would report similar experiences.

Whether the four patients who died would have done so anyway is impossible to answer; there is no doubt that their management was not ideal. What we report is directly related to bed closures, nursing shortages, and medical patients being admitted into surgical or gynaecological wards. These patients often do not get the attention they should, and junior doctors may spend hours on the telephone trying to find a bed, which is not part of their duties. It is just not true for politicians to assert that all in the garden is rosy and that using money as the sole measure of success is hopeless and dishonest.

This report shows that 11% of our acute admissions were not dealt with properly and that this is not the result of poor medical skills or overworked house staff; it relates directly to the shortages of beds and appropriate equipment. Compared with the overall admissions for the period these cases were in the same diagnostic categories. The numbers are, however, too few for statistical analysis.

There is shortly to be a new hospital built on this site but the number of beds for acutely ill patients will not really increase. We constantly hear that the population changes will balance out with the facilities offered in the hospitals. This is fantasy, and if the future hospital service is to be like that of the past five years then it bodes ill for those living in our part of London. It is far better to have some empty beds, leaving a little leeway, rather than to try running hospitals at 100% occupancy, which is what we do now. We have considerable fears for the future and wait to see how the new white paper affects patient care. On casual perusal much of it seems irrelevant to the problems we encounter and have reported.

E N COOMES
J M HARRISON

St Stephen's Hospital,
London SW10 9TH

Sir,—The government's white paper suggests that health authorities will be encouraged to purchase services both across area boundaries and in the private sector for an agreed fee.

The ear, nose, and throat unit at St Bartholomew's Hospital, London, cannot readily handle the demand for tonsillectomy in the catchment areas of the City and Hackney and Newham Health Authorities. After the allocation of central Department of Health and Social Security funding in 1987 and 1988 to reduce waiting lists the unit had two "tonsillectomy blitzes," whereby at an all in unit cost per patient we hired private facilities. In 1987 an arrangement was negotiated with the Princess Grace Hospital, London, in which a fee of £180 per patient was paid to cover all inpatient costs including fees for theatre, drugs, pathology and blood transfusion services, and overnight stay.

After the success of the first blitz a second sum was allocated from central funding in 1988. Tenders were invited from various local private hospitals and those shortlisted were required to arrange sufficient nursing staff to make available two operating theatres for our exclusive use, provide recovery facilities, and permit access to intensive care in an emergency. It was agreed that any patient requiring inpatient care after the weekend would be transferred to St Bartholomew's. The London Independent Hospital offered the most attractive terms of £150 unit cost per patient.

Consultants at the unit and consultant anaesthetists from St Bartholomew's provided free senior cover, and a contribution to their respective departmental funds was negotiated. Extra duty payments were made to the junior medical staff concerned. These costs were subtracted from the total sum available and divided by the unit cost per patient to give the maximum number of patients who could be included in each project, which was 128 in 1987 and 152 in 1988.

Preadmission screening clinics and an efficient reserve list were organised to ensure that the target of 280 cases was achieved, a measure of success which contrasts with the high non-attendance rate for NHS elective operations. We think that this reflects in part the fact that we were confined to a specific limited budget so that any failure to operate on the specified number of patients would entail a waste of money. Clearly, the interaction of the NHS and the private sector was mutually beneficial in this instance.

R D R McRAE
D J GATLAND
M H KEENE

Ear, Nose, and Throat Department,
St Bartholomew's Hospital, London EC1A 7BE

Sir,—Watching *Panorama* on 13 March, I was pleased to hear, at last, a balanced appraisal of the white paper *Working for Patients*.

I have been disappointed to have only the negative views of the BMA presented to me through the two news sheets and *BMA News Review*. I cannot believe that the white paper has nothing of merit in it, and I regret that the association has seen fit to present such a biased opinion. In particular the attitude to general practitioners holding their own budgets is particularly sad, suggesting that this will inevitably lead to second class medicine and a second rate service to patients.

I work in a large district general hospital radiology department with a budget of £1m and a throughput of 120 000 examinations a year. We are no strangers to budgets: we have had budget restriction, our surplus taken to pay off the debts of other departments, and the following year's budget pruned accordingly. Despite this we have expanded our service, increased our staffing, upgraded our departmental computer, and replaced much of the old office equipment. To do this we have looked at every item of expenditure, from intravenous contrast and barium enema bags to silver recovery from processors; we have identified unnecessary radiography—for example, routine preoperative chest radiography —and vetted all requests for contrast radiography, ultrasonography, and computed tomography and all requests from general practitioners to filter out the less clinically relevant requests.

In the past 10 years our workload has increased by about 6% each year overall, but the workload from general practitioners has increased at double this rate. Arguments can be made about "public expectation," "a negative result being most reassuring," etc, but I suspect that putting general practitioners on a budget would not only reduce the excessive rise in workload for our department but also increase their recognition of those in genuine need of radiography.

If our experience of holding a budget is true also for general practitioners they will find many genuine savings without detriment to those in need, and perhaps they will save sufficiently to improve the service to their patients. To suggest that being on a budget is inevitably going to lead to second rate service to patients is insulting to those of us already in this position.

J R PILLING

Norfolk and Norwich Hospital,
Norwich, Norfolk NR1 3SR

SIR,—We would like to point out that the government's policies as stated in *Working for Patients*[1] could have potentially disastrous implications for NHS hospitals in London. Furthermore, if a hospital were to become self governing this might worsen its position.

The financial problems of districts in London have arisen primarily because residents of these districts use acute inpatient services at a rate 50-100% above what their capitation based allocations would permit.[2 3] The extra 3% for the higher costs in London proposed in the white paper will have a negligible impact on the scale of reductions required in acute inpatient care for London residents as London districts will receive capitation based allocations. The hospitals in London mostly treat patients from London, and thus implementing these allocations will mean fierce competition among these hospitals both for the reduced market within London and in their attempts to attract patients from outside.

The NHS hospitals will have to recoup high capital charges[4] (approximate estimates suggest that these may equal their current running costs) and meet the high costs of employing staff in London.[5] Thus they are unlikely to be chosen by districts and general practitioners with practice budgets outside London as the best buy for services for their residents or patients. Similar reasoning may well be applied to the regional services currently based in London teaching hospitals: these could be far more cheaply provided elsewhere. The NHS hospitals would also be poorly placed to compete with private hospitals in London if the private hospitals can meet their capital charges from their private patients and price the services that they offer in competition with the NHS at marginal costs.

The effect of the government's proposed policies on London would be to put its districts in a position analogous to that of countries trading in a world recession, where protectionism is a common response. A London district might therefore seek to maximise care provided for its residents by its own hospital: by, for example, making contracts based on reductions in the core services to be provided for its residents by other hospitals. General practitioners and patients may, however, continue to use services as before, which will result in dispute over the standing of contractual obligations.

If a London hospital opted to be self governing it would then have greater freedom to pay its staff more and borrow capital.[6] But is it sensible to introduce such competition for staff? Given the dramatic decline in school leavers, all NHS hospitals will face problems in recruitment. Allowing a few hospitals to pay more than standard rates may help them solve their problem, but only at the expense of others. In London, particularly, an inflationary pay spiral could easily follow, which could not be financed and would be likely, therefore, to result ultimately in hospital closures.

Although there are possible advantages for a London hospital in becoming self governing, these have to be set against the lack of a guaranteed market from a district's population. In addition, if it were a teaching hospital what would happen to its service increment for teaching (SIFT)? If this is allocated to the district where the medical school is located the district could conceivably negotiate teaching arrangements elsewhere. The only way for such a teaching hospital to survive through self government might be to realise its capital assets and move away from London. Would this long term solution gain the support of doctors with

private practice in London? What impact would this upheaval have on training of medical students and research?

R G BEVAN
W W HOLLAND
N B MAYS

Department of Community Medicine,
United Medical and Dental Schools of
  Guy's and St Thomas's Hospitals,
St Thomas's Campus,
London SE1 7EH

1 Secretaries of State for Health, Wales, Northern Ireland, and Scotland. *Working for patients.* London: HMSO, 1989. (Cmnd 555.)
2 Craig M. Estimating the resources required to train medical students and provide services: a survey of English teaching authorities. *Financial Accountability and Management* 1987;3: 135-45.
3 Bevan G, Brazier J. Financial incentives of subregional RAWP. *Br Med J* 1987;295:836-8.
4 Department of Health. *Capital charges.* London: HMSO, 1989.
5 Brazier J. Reviewing RAWP: accounting for cross-boundary flows. *Br Med J* 1987;295:898-900.
6 Department of Health. *Self-governing hospitals.* London: HMSO, 1989.

SIR,—In view of the enormous increase in the information that we expect to receive from the information revolution proposed in the white paper, I though I ought to let you know of the current state of affairs as regards information for plastic surgery.

A patient recently asked me where he could obtain the quickest plastic surgical appointment. My secretary rang the Department of Health, which told us that it did not have the information. My patient wrote to the department, which suggested that he should write to the various regional health authorities in England to give him a list.

I asked him to do so; the results are presented in the table. The information took my secretary, me, and my patient about three months to accumulate. I am now fearful that in future we will have to write to each individual region and hospital

Waiting lists for plastic surgery in regional and district health authorities in England

	Waiting time (weeks*)
South West Thames:	
Queen Mary's Hospital ⎫ Roehampton	2-5
St George's Hospital ⎭	4
East Anglian†	
Mersey:	
Outpatient	21
Inpatient	69
West Midlands†:	
Dudley	6-24
North Warwickshire	9-10
Coventry and Warwickshire Hospital	5-20
North East Thames	> 16 months
South East Thames:	
King's College Hospital	0-33
Surgery	20
Guy's Hospital	0-5
Surgery	107
Salisbury	12
Surgery	2 years
North West Thames	27·5 months

*Unless stated otherwise.
†Doctor asked to write for information.

to find out not only their waiting lists but also the particular costs of each treatment that we require for our patients.

DAVID STEPHENS

London SE24 8SX

Privatisation

SIR,—The outcome of the government's recent review of the NHS will not be clear for some years but there is one particularly alarming section (2.24)

The Royal College of General Practitioners and the BMA are united in their views on two white papers: on general practice and on the NHS itself

GENERAL PRACTITIONER

concerning a new system for charging for capital in the NHS.[1] Health authorities will be charged for existing and future capital assets: "The charging system will provide a strong incentive for every authority to use its assets efficiently and to invest wisely. It will also place NHS hospitals on a more level footing with private hospitals, which have to meet the cost of capital on a normal commercial basis."

Surely this statement can mean only one thing: after the initiation of the proposals set out in *Working for Patients* and once Mrs Thatcher has established her fourth administration in 1991 NHS hospitals will be instructed to compete directly with private hospitals. I assume by then Mr Clarke will have changed his job so that his successor will not be bound by the present Secretary of State's protests that there are no privatisation plans. Worse, the authors of the white paper still clearly consider that "the NHS is safe in our hands" as it is at present and more so as a result of the review. The privatisation of water and electricity, unappealing as they are, fade into obscurity by contrast with this plan to undermine the best health service on the globe. For which party do I vote next?

ROGER GABRIEL

Renal Unit,
St Mary's Hospital,
London W2 1NY

1 Department of Health. *Working for patients.* London: HMSO, 1989:18.

SIR,—The new white paper describes a service that puts patients first, but these will be mainly private patients.

We all welcome shorter waiting lists, better hospital services, and the freedom to choose our general practitioner. Is this, however, what is really being offered? Based on information from higher management this document, in fact, lays down the foundations for a two tier service.

The fundamental facts regarding the money to be made available for the new health service have not been made public; this information is crucial in determining the extent of the proposed changes.

If implemented two key proposals will make a

two tier service inevitable: the establishment of general practices with their own NHS budgets and the creation of self governing hospitals or trusts. These proposals are closely linked, and they provide the foundations for an alternative service funded by private insurance.

It is clear to many of our managers that there will be no appreciable increase in government funding to the NHS. For example, the Riverside district in London now receives £150m a year. In future if the white paper is implemented it will receive only £75m a year plus a possible 5% to account for the special needs of the population (according to calculations by the district's management based on its population figures) to finance already severely cut hospital services, general practitioners whose practices do not hold their own NHS budgets, and the community services, which are thoroughly neglected in the white paper. Such a reduction leaves little room for real improvements in the government funded health services.

Failure to increase the funding of the NHS, the main area of savings for this district and its regional health authority as well as for others, will result in as many people as possible being encouraged to take out private insurance schemes to free money for poorer patients. The main effect of the white paper will be to produce more private patients by the implementation of the two key proposals.

Self governing hospitals will have no public funding and will have to make their money by selling their services on the free market. Profitable services are cold surgery, oncology, and a few other select services. The hospitals will not make money from mentally ill, chronically ill, and old patients; the services to these populations will have to be financed by district health authorities. Potential customers of self governing hospitals initially may be NHS patients referred by their general practitioners, who are trying to choose the best for them.

According to economic studies in the United States and elsewhere, however, market forces will increase the prices of these specialist services because they will be sold to the highest bidder. The fact is that no private or national health service offers such a good service for so little money with only about 2·9% of the country's gross national product. In all private health services the cost of health care rises to over 10% of the gross national product. So with time general practitioners will be able to send only their private patients to the centres of excellence in self governing hospitals whereas their NHS patients will have to go where treatment is cheaper.

In practices that remain directly funded by the district health authority NHS patients will be sent to the hospital of the district's choice, a decision more likely to be dictated by limited resources than by quality of services as the same district will also be paying for the care of more old and chronically ill people.

As for the general practices with NHS budgets, their doctors will have to select whom they take on to their lists despite government statements to the contrary. The trusting relationship that exists between most good general practitioners and their patients will be destroyed as no NHS patient will ever be sure whether he or she is getting the best treatment or the most economical one.

Neither my district manager nor most of my colleagues can see how the self governing hospitals will differ from private hospitals in that they will have the greatest possible freedom to run their own affairs as long as they remain financially sound. We also cannot find any clear indications in the working papers how medical training and research will be organised or funded.

The remarkable lack of figures on the financing of the new service in the white paper makes the proposals unacceptable. This government does not have an electoral mandate to change the nature of the health service, which should remain, in principle and in practice, free and accessible to all. If our health service is to change then we have the right to know the truth.

FELICITY DE ZULUETA

London N6 6JJ

SIR,—Dr Stephen Lock poses the question "...at a time when large scale privatisation is underway can that of the NHS be far behind?"[1] I would like to suggest that it is already taking place, albeit under a different name.

Exeter Health Authority has long been an avid proponent of community care. The district general manager and director of social services have said "it is the front line staff who best know what it is will enable their clients to remain in the community—where everyone wants to be" and "our thanks to all the staff who have cooperated in closing the old mental hospitals, so releasing the human and financial resources which have made it possible to do more and better things for people in the community."[2]

Between 1984 and 1988 psychogeriatric beds within the district fell from 289 to 144, a loss of 145, and local authority part III accommodation also fell from 835 to 825, a loss of 12. During the same period the number of private beds for the elderly rose from 1963 to 2835, a massive increase of 972 places. This means that over the five years the number of elderly people living in registered institutions rose by 815, all of which are in the private sector. Our district is expected to realise in excess of £40m from the sale of its two mental hospitals, and we now know that much of this money will be diverted from mental health.

Though I am a supporter of community care, much of what is happening seems to reflect a shift of the human and financial burden of care from the health authority towards the private sector. In my more cynical moments I wonder whether the main reason for the rapid thrust into the community of services for psychiatric patients, those with mental handicap, and the elderly is simply that these sections of the population are least likely to complain about what is happening.

I believe that it is time that the Department of Health and some districts became more open about the aims underlying their policies.

MARTIN BRISCOE

Wonford House Hospital,
Wonford,
Exeter EX2 5AF

1 Lock S. Steaming through the NHS. *Br Med J* 1989;**298**:619-20. (11 March.)
2 Exeter Health Authority. *The first year of the Courtney scheme 1988.* Exeter: Exeter Health Authority, 1988.

Funding

SIR,—That the white paper is about keeping costs under control rather than quality of care is shown by the following examples.

Firstly, 100 new consultant posts in the next three years to reduce junior staff workloads is nonsense. That means 33 new posts a year or one new post for every 60 NHS hospitals, of which there are about 2000. Fifty nine out of 60 hospitals will not see even one new consultant. How can that reduce workloads?

Secondly, the white paper claims that it wants a better service. On the other hand, it says that general practitioners should be encouraged to take on more patients. These two ideas are incompatible; more patients mean shorter consultation times and a lowering of standards.

Thirdly, it wants good general practitioners to earn more by attracting more patients. Yet everyone knows that the list size is bound to fall as the population is not growing though the number of general practitioners is. A few general practitioners will manage to get more patients, but on the whole it will not be because they are good but because their area is short of doctors. We will have lost on our basic practice allowance without making up for it from any increase in list size and items of service. In other words, the government's true intention is to reduce gradually the average income of general practitioners.

Fourthly, it says that large practices will be given the opportunity to save money from their budgets, when its real intention is to tighten the budget gradually until there is no more saving to be made. These practices may save money for themselves but only for a short period.

The real aim of the white paper is cost cutting: quality is only secondary.

GUY AH-MOYE

London SW16 3AZ

SIR,—An important factor in initiating the NHS review was the successful campaign highlighting shortfalls in NHS funding. In the debate about the white paper[1] the level of funding is being neglected. Yet this is the acid test of the government's commitment to the NHS.

In a well funded system, and with some modifications to the white paper's proposals, district health authorities and general practitioner budget holders can be envisaged acting as true advocates for the people they serve. Services would not simply be bought on the basis of cost but on that of assessed local needs, user friendliness, convenience, quality, and so on. In a poorly funded system, however, cost will inevitably be the overriding factor in determining which services are purchased where. Flexibility and choice will be reduced.

In addition, the doctor-patient relationship stands to be severely damaged, not least because the natural tendency will be to blame the decreased choice on those buying the services—for example, general practitioner budget holders—rather than the government providing the budget.

The government's spending plans for the next three years[2] give little cause for optimism. The cash increase for hospital and community services in 1991-2 over 1990-1 is only 3·5%; for family practitioner services it is 7·3%. Not only are these increases likely to be below the level of general inflation but they fail to recognise that the white paper's proposals are likely to be more expensive to run than the current system. There will, for example, be an increased need for information technology and managerial and accounting services. So at the time when the proposals are coming into full effect NHS finances will be appreciably squeezed. Such considerations support the view that in the long run the government will be happy to see the demand side of the proposed internal market fail, thus providing the opportunity to introduce an insurance based system.

Whether or not the existence of such a hidden agenda is accepted, I believe that it is crucial that in the current debate the need for adequate funding is persistently emphasised. This is one way to illuminate the government's true intentions for the future of the NHS.

NIGEL UNWIN

Manchester Royal Infirmary,
Manchester M13 9WL

1 Secretaries of State for Health, Wales, Northern Ireland, and Scotland. *Working for patients.* London: HMSO, 1989. (Cmnd 555.)
2 Treasury. *The government's expenditure plans 1989-90 to 1991-92.* London: HMSO, 1989. (Cmnd 614.)

SIR,—I am surprised that in the present climate of disenchantment with the government's white paper comment has not been made about the synopsis of John Wells's letter.[1] Perhaps it is ecause it is not appreciated how a small percentage annual reduction in funding can rapidly accumulate into a large amount.

With simple arithmetic the following conclusions can be drawn from the facts given in the letter. The average annual growth rate in real spending in the NHS from 1959 to 1979 was ·75%. From 1979 to 1988, the Thatcher years, the increase has been only 1·6%. Let this be compared with the previous five years (under Wilson/Callaghan), when the average annual growth was ·6%. With 1·6% growth £100 of expenditure in 1979 would have increased to £115.36 in 1988. With 3·6% annual growth its value would have increased to £137.48. This represents a shortfall in revenue for 1988 of 19·15%. I am sure that many of the problems of the district health authorities would be solved if their present income was increased by that amount.

Even worse, however, is the accumulated loss of funding over the period. With the same £100 base the total loss in income over those nine years is 103.40, equivalent to a loss of 89·6% of the 1988 annual budget. This will inevitably become rapidly worse over the next few years unless it is corrected immediately.

In connection with the privatisation of the water industry Mrs Thatcher said recently that if better quality was desired it would have to be paid for. If only she would apply the same principles to the NHS.

P S FOX

Scarborough,
North Yorkshire YO12 5DR

1 Minerva. Views. *Br Med J* 1989;**298**:618. (4 March.)

Merit awards

SIR,—The government and review body greatly underestimate the value of late merit awards to the National Health Service. At a time when family commitments are decreasing, the drive of youth is diminishing, and outside interests and commitments in advance of retirement are increasing, the possibility of a further merit award, both for its kudos and for its beneficial effect on pensions, must be a major motivating factor for consultants in their last 10 years of service.

The white paper suggests that merit awards should be reviewable at five year intervals, a move which has many advantages. If this proposal is established many consultants will lose their awards for reasons with which we might sympathise or which may be totally beyond their control, such as declining health. A superannuation will presumably be deducted from the awards, and the consultant will benefit little. Do consultants or their families lose the benefit if death or sudden ill health overtakes them shortly after an award is given but long before their expected retirement?

These potential injustices can be overcome only by allowing a pension to accrue as a result of holding merit awards, irrespective of the time of career at which they are given or withdrawn. This could be done by paying the basic pension at present plus an enhancement for holding merit awards. This could be calculated by dividing the total additional funds required to provide a pension arising from merit awards given to retired consultants by the number of years, adjusted to the level of the award, required to earn them. Enhancement would then be paid to holders of awards under the new system on the basis of the number of years that they had held an award at each level. A similar system would also overcome the injustices that have already arisen from the full super-

annuation of domiciliary consultations, which often decrease in number as consultants become older.

C K CONNOLLY

Friarage Hospital,
Northallerton,
North Yorkshire DL6 1JG

Other perspectives

SIR,—Before the profession gets itself embroiled in a conflict with this most unusual of British governments the British Medical Association had better review the nature of the political situation which has been precipitated by recent ministerial actions.

I have been shocked by the deriding statements of Margaret Thatcher's (or should I say Her Majesty's) ministers at the launch of the so called proposals for National Health Service reform. Comments implying that NHS consultants will need to be "coerced" to treat patients effectively and that general practitioners merely "reach for their wallets" in response to current proposals represent a florid and unequivocal adventure into gutter politics. Most physicians do not have the "street smarts" to undertake such a conflict, and the BMA would be wise not to take on a battle on these terms.

All negotiations can be divided into three separate elements: material issues, procedures, and behaviour. Part of the stock in trade of the dirty tricks brigade is to pull and push the opposition off balance and then set an agenda that places the other side at a disadvantage. Such tactics are, of course, fundamentally antidemocratic and reflect the machinations of a frustrated autocrat who is hoping for a normal physiological rage response to insults and unreasoned proposals.

Thus the medical profession is faced with a much more important issue than merely some proposals for NHS "reform." (Note the word reform, often used for juveniles who have committed offences against society and need remediation and who must submit to social retribution.) The issue which is at the top of the government's hidden agenda is the relationship of the medical profession to the government itself. Clearly the wished for position is that of master and servant. If the BMA undertakes any discussions of material issues at a time of such disgraceful lack of normal negotiation behaviour the overriding issue of whether the profession should submit to an autocratic style will be lost.

Thus no discussion should take place about new or old NHS problems until a proper and appropriate relationship between the profession and the government can be re-established. This should be the BMA's agenda and it will require an icy calmness on behalf of the BMA leadership to achieve this objective. Thus the BMA must move to the high ground and talk about substantive issues only when the government has the stature to return to more traditional methods of doing business.

In the meantime individual doctors and the BMA had better get the media and the public at large to understand the nature of the specific and wider issues at stake. This government is attacking, rather than negotiating with, several professional groups (doctors, lawyers, and teachers) and has tilted against institutions of free speech and those holding alternative political views—for example, the BBC and the Commonwealth of Nations. The fundamental basis of the British constitution is "checks and balances." Ignoring normal channels for consultation and

debate is a clear signal of a drift towards autocracy. Britons watch out.

L PETER FIELDING

Department of Surgery,
Yale University School of Medicine,
St Mary's Hospital,
Waterbury,
CT 06706, USA

SIR,—Management of the NHS by clinicians is presently of great importance for the future. More should perhaps be learnt how management by doctors is carried out in other countries. For example, in Australia is the Royal Australian College of Medical Administrators. Only doctors are eligible for its fellowship, which entails a rigorous examination, requiring in service training together with academic work in law related to medical work, government, staff relationships, financial management, ethics, building maintenance, heating, ventilation, public health, and, indeed, everything to do with medical administration and management.

Educated and trained doctors with the fellowship are invaluable in all areas of medicine. They manage and administer and are found in government offices, in hospitals, and anywhere where a clinical managerial and administrative input is required—that is, everywhere where medicine is practised. In Australia medicine is managed by these trained doctors in concert with others.

It would be well if we could in our own ways follow this example. The remit of our community physicians seems more restricted than that of these medical administrators, whose role is better defined and probably more widely accepted in the whole Australian medical community.

PHILIP RHODES

Brockenhurst, Hampshire SO42 7RH

SIR,—Traditionally, the British Medical Association seems to oppose change of almost any kind. The present generation must be perplexed when they learn that the National Health Service was vigorously attacked at the time of its inception—and tonsils were still being removed on kitchen tables at the time.

To those like myself, a former soldier but then a student, the NHS was a godsend for it removed the dread of having to cost services by appraising the quality of a carpet, the pictures, and the furnishings of an abode.

Now, 40 years later, there is the prospect of belonging to a hospital or practice that can become a citadel of excellence in which the members or partners have the incentive to pursue the highest standards of medicine with the greatest control and to generate revenues to further their endeavours.

The realists in the profession, surely, appreciate that the service cannot be open ended and that some degree of selective constraint and common sense is imperative if we are to perpetuate a universal health service as good as the NHS.

Another group of realists are the housemen and final year students, who, almost to a man (or woman), are heading for general practice in droves, whereas less worldly beings sequestered in the colleges plot exit examinations, further discouraging specialisation and confounding the sensible. No wonder the public are coming to realise that we really are a trades union.

FRANK C WALKER

South Cleveland Hospital,
Middlesbrough,
Cleveland TS4 3BW

NHS review—the first three months

J R Butler

Health Services Research Unit, University of Kent at Canterbury, Canterbury, Kent CT2 7NF
J R Butler, *professor of health services studies*

On the current timetable there will be no chance to evaluate the resource management initiative projects taking place at centres like Newcastle's Freeman Hospital

Much of the style and content of the government's white paper on the NHS was bound to provoke antagonism.[1] Firstly, the timetable requiring the first hospital trusts and budget holding practices to be operational by the end of 1991 is widely regarded as all but impossible. It permits no time for evaluative studies or demonstration projects. Secondly, the government's apparent determination to impose the full set of changes on a reluctant service is abrasive and confrontational. By defending the white paper hook, line, and sinker the government has failed to allow the service to respond to the positive features while seeking further clarification of the more questionable elements.

Thirdly, the vagueness of many of the white paper's proposals does not encourage the belief that their consequences have been carefully anticipated and approved. The absurdly fine detail in which the valuation of capital assets has been described (requiring, for example, the separate valuation of every individual item above £1000) emphasises the paucity of detail supporting innovative proposals such as creating hospital trusts and pricing and selling services. Virtually nothing has been said about the implications of these profound changes for community care, medical manpower planning and training, strategic planning of health care services, management and accounting costs, or pursuit of social and geographical equity in health care. Nowhere has it been explained exactly how patients will have a greater choice of health care at no less inconvenience than at present. All that has been offered are broad assurances that all will be well.

Beneath the justifiable demands for detailed answers to questions such as these are deeper fears about long term objectives and implications. The white paper is to be understood as a political statement, not as a planning document; it seeks to apply to health care many of the principles of change that are being implemented throughout the public sector services. Its effect will be to destabilise the NHS, a process that may be intensified through government policies for the future funding of the service. Although the review was set up amid widespread fears about the underfunding of the NHS, the white paper offers no prospect of change in either the level or the source of funds. Indeed, the 1989 Public Expenditure White Paper,[2]

> "*It is regrettable, however, that the intense hostility engendered by the white paper has obstructed much real debate about its meritorious features.*"

published the day before the white paper, forecast annual increases in total NHS expenditure of only 7·7%, 5·3%, and 4·2% respectively over the next three years. These figures do not allow for inflation, nor do they take account of demographic or technological changes. Circumstances could easily arise (such as the continuation of high inflation) in which these figures would become real cuts.

The destabilisation of the NHS, the absence of increased expenditure, and the introduction of the principle of tax relief on private health insurance premiums have fuelled fears that the proposals are an interim step towards privatisation. Although any such intent has been denied by Mr Clarke, the fear is reasonable. The government believes in the power of market forces to produce an efficient allocation of goods and services, and it has implemented that belief in public services that 10 years ago almost nobody thought could be privatised. There is no reason why this long term political programme should stop short at the NHS.

It is regrettable, however, that the intense hostility engendered by the white paper has obstructed much real debate about its meritorious features. That the hostility has spilt over to the proposed new contract for general practitioners has exacerbated the tendency to simplify and polarise opinion, as though there are no midway points between an uncritical belief in the rightness of the government's proposals and an implacable opposition to every last detail.

Several features of the white paper do reflect and develop ideas that have been discussed for some time and that until recently were regarded as reasonable ways of tackling some of the problems that plainly exist in the NHS. Introducing medical audit, developing better information systems, devolving budgets to doctors whose decisions commit the expenditure of public money, revising the element of cross boundary flows in the RAWP (Resource Allocation Working Party) formula, searching for ways of rewarding rather than

UNIVERSITY OF NEWCASTLE UPON TYNE

> *"Thus it would be wrong to reject parts of the white paper that are merely building on trends already underway without making alternative suggestions for tackling the important problems they deal with . . ."*

penalising productive hospitals, and controlling excessive prescribing are all activities that have been debated for some time, and most have been issues in which doctors have been prominent in pushing for change. The white paper's proposals in these matters may not be sufficiently detailed or wholly practicable, but there should be debate about their merits as instruments of change.

Thus it would be wrong to reject parts of the white paper that are merely building on trends already underway without making alternative suggestions for tackling the important problems they deal with, although the service has not been encouraged to respond critically and selectively to different proposals. But the government should also recognise why its white paper has aroused such antagonism and seek to answer its critics with detailed evidence and argument rather than bland reassurance. The central notion of the internal market might be made to work for the benefit of patients in certain circumstances, but the evidence—for example, from a series of demonstration projects—needs to be assembled before its national introduction. It is with the aim of raising the debate that the *BMJ* has brought together the series of articles into this book. Perhaps the time has come for the posturing to stop and the detailed discussions to start. Otherwise the NHS and those whom it serves may become victims of the verbal cross fire.

1 Secretaries of State for Health, Wales, Northern Ireland, and Scotland. *Working for patients*. London: HMSO, 1989. (Cmnd 555.)
2 HM Treasury. *The government's expenditure plans 1989-90 to 1991-92*. London: HMSO, 1989. (Cmnd 614.)

Pride and prejudice

Stephen Lock *Editor, BMJ*

Aimed at the next election

Where the effect of change is speculative...where the competition rules have not been thought out and we do not know what they will be, where changes almost certainly will not result in better or cheaper health, I believe with all humility that a period of further thought would be the path of wisdom.

Thus Lord Wilberforce, "intellectually brilliant and eminently reasonable," in the debate in the House of Lords.[1] But one change has been made to his speech: he was talking about "advocacy" rather than "health," for the discussion was about the radical changes proposed for the legal professions. The lawyers have won some sort of breathing space; so far the doctors have not—why?

The answer may lie in pride and prejudice. Mr Clarke's pride, his political reputation, is at stake for he was put at the Department of Health to do an impossible job. His short timetable is aimed at the next general election rather than at the public's health, given that introducing the scheme by 1991 will mean the parliamentary draughtsmen having to start work this autumn. Mr Clarke's prejudice comes from too little contact with doctors and nurses—those in daily touch with patients. For, compared with lawyers, few

---

"Something had to be done, but skill was needed to ensure that things became better rather than worse."

---

doctors are MPs or peers, and it is easy to stigmatise the unknown, the health professionals, as unreasonable opponents inevitably and implacably opposed to any change.

The reality is different. The crisis arose out of complaints from the care givers of the long term underfunding of the health service, threatening standards of civilised care. Something had to be done, but skill was needed to ensure that things became better rather than worse. If the reforms were to be radical then debate and experiment would be vital and detail was all important. None of this could be achieved without consulting those who do the work: doctors, nurses, and managers. In the event consultation did not take place, and the plans for the largest industry in Europe became enshrined in 60 000 words of waffle.

If serious discussion was lacking on the government side, it has emerged in the professional comments. Thus not only has our series of articles detailed the impossibly short timetable, the failure to experiment and the lack of information systems but it has also come up with positive suggestions: Professor David Morrell, for example, has shown how in general practice agreed standards together with audit could raise the quality of care without major disturbance.[2][3]

Inevitably, however, complaints and suggestions from the profession will be dismissed as trade union

---

"But the profession should not compromise on the widely agreed major defects of the plans."

---

pleading. So let two sets of knowledgeable outsiders comment. In his recent interview with Richard Smith Professor Alain Enthoven saw several good ideas in the white paper, among them separating the demand and the supply side of the NHS, making money follow patients, and greater local delegation.[4] But he regrets that the government has not chosen to experiment. Given the large changes, the pace of the timetable is amazing, he believes; health care just does not change at that speed.

The second group of comments come from Patricia Day and Rudolf Klein in their evidence to the social services committee. Like Enthoven, they welcome the review's drift, with its insistence on accountability, suggesting that the dangers of a competitive market have been exaggerated. But their real question is "whether all this can be done without demoralising the providers and without destroying the inherited capital of professional dedication." How the proposals are implemented is crucial. Experiments are inevitable, Day and Klein conclude: the best way of convincing conscripts is to show that new ideas work. And to overcome the disruption and threat inevitable in change the government should provide a special budget.

With Mr David Mellor's recent statement about the plans not being tablets of stone some have detected signs of willingness to negotiate. Doctors would well come this, and the major points for debate should emerge at the BMA's special representative meeting on 17 May (the most important for the health of Britain since 1948). Given that the concept of medical audit has come from the profession, for example, they would agree to this as a plank for reorganisation. (I suspect also that they would concede a reasonable date for concluding the principal negotiations.) But they should not compromise on the widely agreed major defects of the plans. The timetable is too short. There have been no experiments. The special needs of the community, teaching, and research have been ignored. And above all there is an absence of detail. The nation's health is too important to be threatened with such ill thought out changes. Nor are the health professionals kulaks to be coerced against their will.

1 Alexander R. True cost of the law reforms. *Independent* 1989 Apr 18:19 (col 4-6).
2 Morrell D. The new general practitioner contract: Is there an alternative? *Br Med J* 1989;**298**: 1005-7.
3 *British Medical Journal. The NHS review—what it means.* London: BMJ, 1989.
4 Smith R. Words from the source: an interview with Alain Enthoven. *Br Med J* 1989;**298**:1166-8.